It's easy. Just pre-pay for 12 hours of driving tuition and we'll give you an additional hour free, plus we will discount your first 12 hours by £24 and give you a £100 holiday voucher*.

Best of all, we're the only national driving school exclusively using fully qualified instructors. And you'll be learning in a Ford Focus with air conditioning and power steering.

Great value. A great instructor. And a great car. You get it all.

*Terms and Conditions apply.

Just AAsk.

AA driving school
0800 60 70 80
www.theAA.com

- - - - - - - - - - - - - - - - - - - -

Free hour when you pre-pay for 12 hours

Complete this voucher and hand it to your instructor at the start of your first lesson.

Name _____

Pupil Number (given on calling 0800 60 70 80) _____

I apply for my one hour of free driving tuition having pre-paid for 12 hours and confirm I am not an existing pupil of AA driving school.

Signed _____

For Instructor Use Only:

Instructor Name _____ Instructor Number _____

Theory BK Car INDEX Bks

AA

THEORY TEST
The *OFFICIAL* Questions & Answers

Produced by AA Publishing.
© Automobile Association Developments Limited 2003
First edition 1996
Reprinted 1996 (5 times)
Second edition with revised questions 1997
Reprinted 1998 (twice)
Third edition with revised questions 1998
Reprinted with amendments 1998 (twice)
Fourth edition with revised questions 1999
Reprinted 2000
Fifth edition with revised questions 2000
Sixth edition with revised questions 2001
Reprinted 2002 (twice) and June 2002 with amendment
Seventh edition with revised questions 2003.
Reprinted Oct 2003
This edition published 2003 for Index Books Limited

ISBN 0 7495 3811 2

Published by AA Publishing (a trading name of Automobile
Association Developments Limited, whose registered office is
Millstream, Maidenhead Road, Windsor, SL4 5GD; registered
number 1878835). A01840

The AA's Web site address is *www.theAA.com*

Colour separation by Keene Group, Andover.
Printed in Portugal by Grafiasa S.A.

While every effort has been made to include the widest possible range of questions available at the time of printing, the Government may from time to time change, add or remove questions, and the publisher cannot be held responsible for questions that may appear on a question paper which were not available for inclusion in this book.

STOP PRESS
The Driving Standards Agency have withdrawn question 803 from the official database of questions. This question will NOT form part of the Theory Test.

Contents

How to use this book

Introduction

You now have to pass two driving tests before you can apply for a full driving licence. The Theory Test was introduced in 1996 to check that drivers know more than just how to operate a car. This book contains the official car questions from the Driving Standards Agency (DSA) that you may have to answer. You will have to pass both the question part and the new video Hazard Perception part to pass your Theory Test, before you can apply for the Practical Test.

The Theory Test consists of 35 questions, and a separate video clips section, called Hazard Perception. You will have 40 minutes to complete the question part of the test, using a touch-screen, and all questions are multiple-choice. You have to score 30 out of 35 on the theory questions to pass. The Government may, from time to time, introduce new or amended questions. However, if you are fully prepared on each topic, you will be in a position to answer any question.

How to use this book

This book contains all the official questions for car drivers which appear in the question bank of the Driving Standards Agency (DSA). You could be tested on any of these questions when you take your touch-screen Theory Test.

The questions in this book are arranged in themes, such as **Safety Margins** and **Hazard Awareness**. Each theme has its own colour band, to help you find your way around. However, it is not cut and dried, and as you start to work through the questions you will soon discover that similar questions on the same topic may appear in different theme sections. Don't be put off by this, but read each question and the choice of answers very carefully. A similar question may be being asked in a different way, in order to test your full understanding.

You'll find all the correct answers to the questions at the back of the book. That way, you can easily test yourself to see what you are getting right, and what you need to work on.

Questions marked with an **NI** symbol are those not found in Theory Test papers in Northern Ireland

How to study for the Theory Test

Remember
- Do not try too many questions at once.
- Do not try to learn the answers by heart.
- The order of the questions in this book may be different from how they are arranged in the actual test – so do not try to memorise the order.

How to answer the questions

Each questions has four, five or six answers. You must mark the boxes with the correct answer or answers. Each question tells you how many answers to mark.

Study each question carefully, making sure you understand what it is asking you. Look carefully at any diagram, drawing or photograph. Before you look at the answers given, decide what you think the right answer may be. You can then select the answer that matches the one you had decided on. If you follow this system, you will avoid being confused by answers that appear to be similar.

Hazard Perception

The video clips element of the Theory Test is known as Hazard Perception. Its aim is to find out how good you are at noticing hazards developing up on the road ahead. The test will also show how much you know about the risks of driving, that is, risks to you as a driver, risks to your passengers and risks to other road users.

What to expect

The test lasts for about 20 minutes. First you will be given some instructions explaining how it works; you will also get a chance to practise with the computer and mouse before you start the test 'for real'. This is to make sure you know what to expect on the test, and that you are happy with what you have to do.

Next you will see film or video clips of real street scenes with traffic such as motor vehicles, pedestrians, cyclists, etc. The scenes are shot from the point of view of a driver in a car. You have to notice hazards that are developing on the road ahead – that is, problems that could lead to an accident. As soon as you notice a hazard developing, click on the mouse control. You will have plenty of time to see the hazard – but the sooner you notice it, the more marks you will score.

Every clip has at least one hazard in it – some clips may have more than one hazard. You currently have to score 44 out of 75 to pass **but** the pass mark may change and it is advisable to check with your driving instructor or the Driving Standards Agency before sitting your test. (Note that the computer has checks built in to show up anyone trying to cheat – for example, someone who keeps clicking the mouse all the time!)

All the film clips have been shot on 'real roads' and contain all sorts of hazards however you will only score points for 'developing' hazards'.

For each hazard you spot you get one or more points. The more quickly you spot the hazard developing on-screen, and click on it with the mouse, the higher your score. But be aware that each test clip will only be shown once. You will not have an opportunity to go back to an earlier clip and change your response, so you need to concentrate.

Remember, you have to pass both the theory questions and hazard perception to pass the Theory Test. At the end of the test they will tell you your scores for both parts. Even if you only failed on one part of the Theory Test, you still have to take both parts again next time.

Preparing for Hazard Perception

Learner drivers need more training in how to spot hazards, because they are often so busy thinking about using the car's controls that they forget to watch the road and traffic. Learner drivers, and new drivers are up to two seconds slower at spotting hazards than more experienced drivers. Proper training can really help you to see more of the hazards that you will meet when driving, and to see those hazards earlier. So you're less likely to have an accident.

So what does Hazard Perception mean?

A hazard is anything that might cause you to change speed or direction when driving. The Hazard Perception element of the Theory Test is about spotting developing hazards. This is one of the key skills of good driving, and is also called anticipation. Anticipating hazards, such as car doors opening or children running into the road, means looking out for them in advance and taking the appropriate action now.

As you get more driving experience you will start to learn about times and places where you are most likely to meet hazards. An example of this is the rush hour. You know that people take more risks when driving in the rush hour. Maybe they have to drop their children off at school before going to work. Maybe they are late for a business meeting or are in a hurry to get home. So you have to be prepared for bad driving, for example other drivers pulling out in front of you.

Much of The Highway Code is about the hazards you find at junctions. You might be on a minor road and have to turn out on to a major road where you can't see clearly both ways; or you might be at a crossroads where there are no signs saying which vehicle has priority (should go first).

Your driving instructor has been trained to help you learn hazard perception skills, and can give you plenty of practice in what to look out for when driving, how to anticipate hazards, and what action to take when you have to deal with hazards of all kinds. You won't be able to practise with the real video clips used in the test, of course, but training books and practice videos will be made available.

Introduction

Preparing for both tests

You are strongly recommended to prepare for the Theory Test at the same time as you develop your skills behind the wheel for the Practical Test. Obviously, there are many similarities between the two tests – it is all about helping to make you a safer driver on today's busy roads. By preparing for both tests at the same time, you will reinforce your knowledge and understanding of all aspects of driving and you will improve your chances of passing both tests first time.

Selecting a driving school

When you select a driving school to teach you the practical skills, make sure they are prepared to advise and help you with the Theory Test. Good driving schools will provide theory practice papers for you to complete before you take the real test. These papers will help you judge your level of knowledge and help with your preparation. Check with friends who have been taught recently, and make sure you understand the difference between an instructor who displays a pink badge or licence (a trainee instructor) and one who displays a green badge or licence (a fully qualified instructor).

Price is important, so find out whether the school offers any discounts for blocks or courses of lessons paid in advance; if you decide to pay in advance, make sure the driving school is reputable. If lesson prices are very low, ask yourself 'why?' Check how long the lesson will last, some driving schools offer lessons of less than 60 minutes. And don't forget to ask about the car you'll be learning to drive in. Is it modern and reliable? Is it insured? Has it dual controls?

As with all courses, there are a number of subjects you will need to master. All good driving schools will have available a progress sheet and syllabus which sets out all the skills you will need and keeps a record of your progress. You will probably find that if you take a two-hour lesson every week, your rate of progress will surprise you!

It is important that you should not take your Theory Test too early in your course of practical lessons. This is because you need the experience of meeting real hazards while you are learning to drive, so that you will be able to pass the Hazard Perception part of the Theory Test. You must pass the Theory Test before you can take the Practical Test. Agree a plan of action with your driving instructor.

After a few hours of driving tuition the instructor will discuss with you a structured course to suit your needs and you can agree on the likely date when you will be ready to take the Practical Test. Once you have passed your Theory Test, you can apply for a Practical Test appointment; this will give you added incentive to prepare thoroughly.

The AA driving school

The AA has a driving school that only uses fully qualified instructors, who are all familiar with the Theory Test, Hazard Perception and the Practical Test. Why not give them a try? You can ring for details on freephone 0800 60 70 80 or visit the website at **www.theAA.com**.

Being a good driver is more than just having the knowledge and the skills – it is about applying them with the right attitude. No one is a 'natural' or a 'perfect driver'. All drivers make mistakes. Being careful, courteous and considerate to other road users will complement the skills and knowledge you will acquire in the coming weeks and make you a good and safe driver.

Further Information

For lots of hints and tips on driving or to take a mock Theory Test visit **www.theAA.com**.

1 Before you make a U-turn in the road, you should

Mark one answer

- [ ] **A.** give an arm signal as well as using your indicators
- [ ] **B.** signal so that other drivers can slow down for you
- [ ] **C.** look over your shoulder for a final check
- [ ] **D.** select a higher gear than normal

2 As you approach this bridge you should

Mark three answers

- [ ] **A.** move into the middle of the road to get a better view
- [ ] **B.** slow down
- [ ] **C.** get over the bridge as quickly as possible
- [ ] **D.** consider using your horn
- [ ] **E.** find another route
- [ ] **F.** beware of pedestrians

3 When following a large vehicle you should keep well back because

Mark one answer

- [ ] **A.** it allows you to corner more quickly
- [ ] **B.** it helps the large vehicle to stop more easily
- [ ] **C.** it allows the driver to see you in the mirrors
- [ ] **D.** it helps you to keep out of the wind

4 In which of these situations should you avoid overtaking?

Mark one answer

- [ ] **A.** Just after a bend
- [ ] **B.** In a one-way street
- [ ] **C.** On a 30mph road
- [ ] **D.** Approaching a dip in the road

5 This road marking warns

Mark one answer

- [ ] **A.** drivers to use the hard shoulder
- [ ] **B.** overtaking drivers there is a bend to the left
- [ ] **C.** overtaking drivers to move back to the left
- [ ] **D.** drivers that it is safe to overtake

6 Your mobile phone rings while you are travelling. You should

Mark one answer

- [ ] **A.** stop immediately
- [ ] **B.** answer it immediately
- [ ] **C.** pull up in a suitable place
- [ ] **D.** pull up at the nearest kerb

TIP Be aware that one in three of road accident fatalities are pedestrians or cyclists.

7 Why are these yellow lines painted across the road?

Mark one answer

- A. To help you choose the correct lane
- B. To help you keep the correct separation distance
- C. To make you aware of your speed
- D. To tell you the distance to the roundabout

8 You are approaching traffic lights that have been on green for some time. You should

Mark one answer

- A. accelerate hard
- B. maintain your speed
- C. be ready to stop
- D. brake hard

9 Which of the following should you do before stopping?

Mark one answer

- A. Sound the horn
- B. Use the mirrors
- C. Select a higher gear
- D. Flash your headlights

10 As a driver what does the term 'Blind Spot' mean?

Mark one answer

- A. An area covered by your right-hand mirror
- B. An area not covered by your headlamps
- C. An area covered by your left-hand mirror
- D. An area not seen in your mirrors

11 Objects hanging from your interior mirror may

Mark two answers

- A. restrict your view
- B. improve your driving
- C. distract your attention
- D. help your concentration

12 Which of the following may cause loss of concentration on a long journey?

Mark four answers

- A. Loud music
- B. Arguing with a passenger
- C. Using a mobile phone
- D. Putting in a cassette tape
- E. Stopping regularly to rest
- F. Pulling up to tune the radio

13 On a long motorway journey boredom can cause you to feel sleepy. You should

Mark two answers

- A. leave the motorway and find a safe place to stop
- B. keep looking around at the surrounding landscape
- C. drive faster to complete your journey sooner
- D. ensure a supply of fresh air into your vehicle
- E. stop on the hard shoulder for a rest

14 You are driving at dusk. You should switch your lights on

Mark two answers

- A. even when street lights are not lit
- B. so others can see you
- C. only when others have done so
- D. only when street lights are lit

15 You are most likely to lose concentration when driving if you

Mark two answers

- A. use a mobile phone
- B. listen to very loud music
- C. switch on the heated rear window
- D. look at the door mirrors

16 Which FOUR are most likely to cause you to lose concentration while you are driving?

Mark four answers

- A. Using a mobile phone
- B. Talking into a microphone
- C. Tuning your car radio
- D. Looking at a map
- E. Checking the mirrors
- F. Using the demisters

17 You should not use a mobile phone whilst driving

Mark one answer

- A. until you are satisfied that no other traffic is near
- B. unless you are able to drive one handed
- C. because it might distract your attention from the road ahead
- D. because reception is poor when the engine is running

18 Your vehicle is fitted with a hands-free phone system. Using this equipment whilst driving

Mark one answer

- A. is quite safe as long as you slow down
- B. could distract your attention from the road
- C. is recommended by *The Highway Code*
- D. could be very good for road safety

19 Using a hands-free phone is likely to

Mark one answer

- A. improve your safety
- B. increase your concentration
- C. reduce your view
- D. divert your attention

20 You should ONLY use a mobile phone when

Mark one answer

- A. receiving a call
- B. suitably parked
- C. driving at less than 30mph
- D. driving an automatic vehicle

21 Using a mobile phone while you are driving

Mark one answer

- A. is acceptable in a vehicle with power steering
- B. will reduce your field of vision
- C. could distract your attention from the road
- D. will affect your vehicle's electronic systems

22 What is the safest way to use a mobile phone in your vehicle?

Mark one answer

- A. Use hands-free equipment
- B. Find a suitable place to stop
- C. Drive slowly on a quiet road
- D. Direct your call through the operator

23 You are driving on a wet road. You have to stop your vehicle in an emergency. You should

Mark one answer

- A. apply the handbrake and footbrake together
- B. keep both hands on the wheel
- C. select reverse gear
- D. give an arm signal

24 When you are moving off from behind a parked car you should

Mark three answers

- A. look round before you move off
- B. use all the mirrors on the vehicle
- C. look round after moving off
- D. use the exterior mirrors only
- E. give a signal if necessary
- F. give a signal after moving off

25 You are travelling along this narrow country road. When passing the cyclist you should go

Mark one answer

- A. slowly, sounding the horn as you pass
- B. quickly, leaving plenty of room
- C. slowly, leaving plenty of room
- D. quickly, sounding the horn as you pass

26 Your vehicle is fitted with a hand-held telephone. To use the telephone you should

Mark one answer

- A. reduce your speed
- B. find a safe place to stop
- C. steer the vehicle with one hand
- D. be particularly careful at junctions

27 To answer a call on your mobile phone while travelling you should

Mark one answer

- A. reduce your speed wherever you are
- B. stop in a proper and convenient place
- C. keep the call time to a minimum
- D. slow down and allow others to overtake

TIP When following long vehicles, keep well back so that you are visible in the driver's mirrors. Take a look at the markers on the sides and the end. They are there to warn you of the length of the vehicle, and sometimes overhanging loads.

28 Your mobile phone rings while you are on the motorway. Before answering you should

Mark one answer   **NI**

- A. reduce your speed to 50mph
- B. pull up on the hard shoulder
- C. move into the left-hand lane
- D. stop in a safe place

29 You are turning right on to a dual carriageway. What should you do before emerging?

Mark one answer

- A. Stop, apply the handbrake and then select a low gear
- B. Position your vehicle well to the left of the side road
- C. Check that the central reserve is wide enough for your vehicle
- D. Make sure that you leave enough room for a following vehicle

30 You lose your way on a busy road. What is the best action to take?

Mark one answer

- A. Stop at traffic lights and ask pedestrians
- B. Shout to other drivers to ask them the way
- C. Turn into a side road, stop and check a map
- D. Check a map, and keep going with the traffic flow

31 You are waiting to emerge from a junction. The screen pillar is restricting your view. What should you be particularly aware of?

Mark one answer

- A. Lorries
- B. Buses
- C. Motorcyclists
- D. Coaches

32 When emerging from junctions which is most likely to obstruct your view?

Mark one answer

- A. Windscreen pillars
- B. Steering wheel
- C. Interior mirror
- D. Windscreen wipers

33 Windscreen pillars can obstruct your view. You should take particular care when

Mark one answer

- A. driving on a motorway
- B. driving on a dual carriageway
- C. approaching a one-way street
- D. approaching bends and junctions

34 You cannot see clearly behind when reversing. What should you do?

Mark one answer

- A. Open your window to look behind
- B. Open the door and look behind
- C. Look in the nearside mirror
- D. Ask someone to guide you

35 **At a pelican crossing the flashing amber light means you MUST**

Mark one answer

- **A.** stop and wait for the green light
- **B.** stop and wait for the red light
- **C.** give way to pedestrians waiting to cross
- **D.** give way to pedestrians already on the crossing

36 **You should never wave people across at pedestrian crossings because**

Mark one answer

- **A.** there may be another vehicle coming
- **B.** they may not be looking
- **C.** it is safer for you to carry on
- **D.** they may not be ready to cross

37 **At a puffin crossing what colour follows the green signal?**

Mark one answer

- **A.** Steady red
- **B.** Flashing amber
- **C.** Steady amber
- **D.** Flashing green

38 **You could use the 'Two-Second Rule'**

Mark one answer

- **A.** before restarting the engine after it has stalled
- **B.** to keep a safe gap from the vehicle in front
- **C.** before using the 'Mirror-Signal-Manoeuvre' routine
- **D.** when emerging on wet roads

39 **'Tailgating' means**

Mark one answer

- **A.** using the rear door of a hatchback car
- **B.** reversing into a parking space
- **C.** following another vehicle too closely
- **D.** driving with rear fog lights on

40 **Following this vehicle too closely is unwise because**

Mark one answer

- **A.** your brakes will overheat
- **B.** your view ahead is increased
- **C.** your engine will overheat
- **D.** your view ahead is reduced

41 **You are following a vehicle on a wet road. You should leave a time gap of at least**

Mark one answer

- **A.** one second
- **B.** two seconds
- **C.** three seconds
- **D.** four seconds

42 **You are in a line of traffic. The driver behind you is following very closely. What action should you take?**

Mark one answer

- **A.** Ignore the following driver and continue to drive within the speed limit
- **B.** Slow down, gradually increasing the gap between you and the vehicle in front
- **C.** Signal left and wave the following driver past
- **D.** Move over to a position just left of the centre line of the road

43 A long, heavily laden lorry is taking a long time to overtake you. What should you do?

Mark one answer

- **A.** Speed up
- **B.** Slow down
- **C.** Hold your speed
- **D.** Change direction

44 Which of the following vehicles will use blue flashing beacons?

Mark three answers

- **A.** Motorway maintenance
- **B.** Bomb disposal
- **C.** Blood transfusion
- **D.** Police patrol
- **E.** Breakdown recovery

45 Which THREE of these emergency services might have blue flashing beacons?

Mark three answers

- **A.** Coastguard
- **B.** Bomb disposal
- **C.** Gritting lorries
- **D.** Animal ambulances
- **E.** Mountain rescue
- **F.** Doctors' cars

46 When being followed by an ambulance showing a flashing blue beacon you should

Mark one answer

- **A.** pull over as soon as safely possible to let it pass
- **B.** accelerate hard to get away from it
- **C.** maintain your speed and course
- **D.** brake harshly and immediately stop in the road

47 What type of emergency vehicle is fitted with a green flashing beacon?

Mark one answer

- **A.** Fire engine
- **B.** Road gritter
- **C.** Ambulance
- **D.** Doctor's car

48 A flashing green beacon on a vehicle means

Mark one answer

- **A.** police on non-urgent duties
- **B.** doctor on an emergency call
- **C.** road safety patrol operating
- **D.** gritting in progress

49 A vehicle has a flashing green beacon. What does this mean?

Mark one answer

- **A.** A doctor is answering an emergency call
- **B.** The vehicle is slow moving
- **C.** It is a motorway police patrol vehicle
- **D.** A vehicle is carrying hazardous chemicals

50 Diamond-shaped signs give instructions to

Mark one answer

- **A.** tram drivers
- **B.** bus drivers
- **C.** lorry drivers
- **D.** taxi drivers

TIP *The Highway Code advises you not to use your mobile if you have an accident on a motorway. Use the (free) emergency phone; it connects directly with the police, who will then be able to identify your exact location.*

51 On a road where trams operate, which of these vehicles will be most at risk from the tram rails?

Mark one answer
- [ ] **A.** Cars
- [ ] **B.** Cycles
- [ ] **C.** Buses
- [ ] **D.** Lorries

52 What should you use your horn for?

Mark one answer
- [ ] **A.** To alert others to your presence
- [ ] **B.** To allow you right of way
- [ ] **C.** To greet other road users
- [ ] **D.** To signal your annoyance

53 You are in a one-way street and want to turn right. You should position yourself

Mark one answer
- [ ] **A.** in the right-hand lane
- [ ] **B.** in the left-hand lane
- [ ] **C.** in either lane, depending on the traffic
- [ ] **D.** just left of the centre line

54 You wish to turn right ahead. Why should you take up the correct position in good time?

Mark one answer
- [ ] **A.** To allow other drivers to pull out in front of you
- [ ] **B.** To give a better view into the road that you're joining
- [ ] **C.** To help other road users know what you intend to do
- [ ] **D.** To allow drivers to pass you on the right

55 At which type of crossing are cyclists allowed to ride across with pedestrians?

Mark one answer
- [ ] **A.** Toucan
- [ ] **B.** Puffin
- [ ] **C.** Pelican
- [ ] **D.** Zebra

56 A bus is stopped at a bus stop ahead of you. Its right-hand indicator is flashing. You should

Mark one answer
- [ ] **A.** flash your headlights and slow down
- [ ] **B.** slow down and give way if it is safe to do so
- [ ] **C.** sound your horn and keep going
- [ ] **D.** slow down and then sound your horn

57 You are travelling at the legal speed limit. A vehicle comes up quickly behind, flashing its headlights. You should

Mark one answer
- [ ] **A.** accelerate to make a gap behind you
- [ ] **B.** touch the brakes sharply to show your brake lights
- [ ] **C.** maintain your speed to prevent the vehicle from overtaking
- [ ] **D.** allow the vehicle to overtake

58 You should ONLY flash your headlights to other road users

Mark one answer

- A. to show that you are giving way
- B. to show that you are about to turn
- C. to tell them that you have right of way
- D. to let them know that you are there

59 You are approaching unmarked crossroads. How should you deal with this type of junction?

Mark one answer

- A. Accelerate and keep to the middle
- B. Slow down and keep to the right
- C. Accelerate looking to the left
- D. Slow down and look both ways

60 You are approaching a pelican crossing. The amber light is flashing. You MUST

Mark one answer

- A. give way to pedestrians who are crossing
- B. encourage pedestrians to cross
- C. not move until the green light appears
- D. stop even if the crossing is clear

61 At puffin crossings which light will not show to a driver?

Mark one answer

- A. Flashing amber
- B. Red
- C. Steady amber
- D. Green

62 A two-second gap between yourself and the car in front is sufficient when conditions are

Mark one answer

- A. wet
- B. good
- C. damp
- D. foggy

63 You are driving on a clear night. There is a steady stream of oncoming traffic. The national speed limit applies. Which lights should you use?

Mark one answer

- A. Full beam headlights
- B. Sidelights
- C. Dipped headlights
- D. Fog lights

64 You are driving behind a large goods vehicle. It signals left but steers to the right. You should

Mark one answer

- A. slow down and let the vehicle turn
- B. drive on, keeping to the left
- C. overtake on the right of it
- D. hold your speed and sound your horn

TIP Remember O A P:
Observe
Anticipate
Plan

65 You are driving along this road. The red van cuts in close in front of you. What should you do?

Mark one answer

- [ ] **A.** Accelerate to get closer to the red van
- [ ] **B.** Give a long blast on the horn
- [ ] **C.** Drop back to leave the correct separation distance
- [ ] **D.** Flash your headlights several times

66 You are waiting in a traffic queue at night. To avoid dazzling following drivers you should

Mark one answer

- [ ] **A.** apply the handbrake only
- [ ] **B.** apply the footbrake only
- [ ] **C.** switch off your headlights
- [ ] **D.** use both the handbrake and footbrake

67 You are driving in traffic at the speed limit for the road. The driver behind is trying to overtake. You should

Mark one answer

- [ ] **A.** move closer to the car ahead, so the driver behind has no room to overtake
- [ ] **B.** wave the driver behind to overtake when it is safe
- [ ] **C.** keep a steady course and allow the driver behind to overtake
- [ ] **D.** accelerate to get away from the driver behind

68 You are driving at night on an unlit road following a slower-moving vehicle. You should

Mark one answer

- [ ] **A.** flash your headlights
- [ ] **B.** use dipped beam headlights
- [ ] **C.** switch off your headlights
- [ ] **D.** use full beam headlights

69 A bus lane on your left shows no times of operation. This means it is

Mark one answer

- [ ] **A.** not in operation at all
- [ ] **B.** only in operation at peak times
- [ ] **C.** in operation 24 hours a day
- [ ] **D.** only in operation in daylight hours

70 You are driving along a country road. A horse and rider are approaching. What should you do?

Mark two answers

- [ ] **A.** Increase your speed
- [ ] **B.** Sound your horn
- [ ] **C.** Flash your headlights
- [ ] **D.** Drive slowly past
- [ ] **E.** Give plenty of room
- [ ] **F.** Rev your engine

71 A person herding sheep asks you to stop. You should

Mark one answer

- A. ignore them as they have no authority
- B. stop and switch off your engine
- C. continue on but drive slowly
- D. try and get past quickly

72 When overtaking a horse and rider you should

Mark one answer

- A. sound your horn as a warning
- B. go past as quickly as possible
- C. flash your headlights as a warning
- D. go past slowly and carefully

73 You are approaching a zebra crossing. Pedestrians are waiting to cross. You should

Mark one answer

- A. give way to the elderly and infirm only
- B. slow down and prepare to stop
- C. use your headlights to indicate they can cross
- D. wave at them to cross the road

74 You are driving a slow-moving vehicle on a narrow winding road. You should

Mark one answer

- A. keep well out to stop vehicles overtaking dangerously
- B. wave following vehicles past you if you think they can overtake quickly
- C. pull in safely when you can, to let following vehicles overtake
- D. give a left signal when it is safe for vehicles to overtake you

75 You are driving a slow-moving vehicle on a narrow road. When traffic wishes to overtake you should

Mark one answer

- A. take no action
- B. put your hazard warning lights on
- C. stop immediately and wave it on
- D. pull in safely as soon as you can do so

76 You are driving a slow-moving vehicle on a narrow winding road. In order to let other vehicles overtake you should

Mark one answer

- A. wave to them to pass
- B. pull in when you can
- C. show a left turn signal
- D. keep left and hold your speed

77 A vehicle pulls out in front of you at a junction. What should you do?

Mark one answer

- A. Swerve past it and sound your horn
- B. Flash your headlights and drive up close behind
- C. Slow down and be ready to stop
- D. Accelerate past it immediately

78 You stop for pedestrians waiting to cross at a zebra crossing. They do not start to cross. What should you do?

Mark one answer

- A. Be patient and wait
- B. Sound your horn
- C. Carry on
- D. Wave them to cross

79 You are following this lorry. You should keep well back from it to

Mark one answer

- [ ] **A.** give you a good view of the road ahead
- [ ] **B.** stop following traffic from rushing through the junction
- [ ] **C.** prevent traffic behind you from overtaking
- [ ] **D.** allow you to hurry through the traffic lights if they change

80 You are approaching a red light at a puffin crossing. Pedestrians are on the crossing. The red light will stay on until

Mark one answer

- [ ] **A.** you start to edge forward on to the crossing
- [ ] **B.** the pedestrians have reached a safe position
- [ ] **C.** the pedestrians are clear of the front of your vehicle
- [ ] **D.** a driver from the opposite direction reaches the crossing

81 Which instrument panel warning light would show that headlights are on full beam?

Mark one answer

- [ ] **A.**
- [ ] **B.**

- [ ] **C.**
- [ ] **D.**

TIP Blue flashing lights are used by ambulances, fire engines and police vehicles, as well as other emergency services Doctors on call display green flashing lights. Gritting lorries, motorway maintenance and breakdown recovery vehicles display flashing amber lights.

82 Which of these, if allowed to get low, could cause an accident?

Mark one answer

- [ ] **A.** Antifreeze level
- [ ] **B.** Brake fluid level
- [ ] **C.** Battery water level
- [ ] **D.** Radiator coolant level

83 Which TWO are badly affected if the tyres are under-inflated?

Mark two answers

- [ ] **A.** Braking
- [ ] **B.** Steering
- [ ] **C.** Changing gear
- [ ] **D.** Parking

84 Motor vehicles can harm the environment. This has resulted in

Mark three answers

- [ ] **A.** air pollution
- [ ] **B.** damage to buildings
- [ ] **C.** reduced health risks
- [ ] **D.** improved public transport
- [ ] **E.** less use of electrical vehicles
- [ ] **F.** using up natural resources

85 Excessive or uneven tyre wear can be caused by faults in which THREE?

Mark three answers

- [ ] **A.** The gearbox
- [ ] **B.** The braking system
- [ ] **C.** The accelerator
- [ ] **D.** The exhaust system
- [ ] **E.** Wheel alignment
- [ ] **F.** The suspension

86 You must NOT sound your horn

Mark one answer

- [ ] **A.** between 10pm and 6am in a built-up area
- [ ] **B.** at any time in a built-up area
- [ ] **C.** between 11.30pm and 7am in a built-up area
- [ ] **D.** between 11.30pm and 6am on any road

87 The pictured vehicle is 'environmentally friendly' because it

Mark three answers

- [ ] **A.** reduces noise pollution
- [ ] **B.** uses diesel fuel
- [ ] **C.** uses electricity
- [ ] **D.** uses unleaded fuel
- [ ] **E.** reduces parking spaces
- [ ] **F.** reduces town traffic

88 Supertrams or Light Rapid Transit (LRT) systems are environmentally friendly because

Mark one answer

- [ ] **A.** they use diesel power
- [ ] **B.** they use quieter roads
- [ ] **C.** they use electric power
- [ ] **D.** they do not operate during rush hour

> **TIP** Large dogs should be in a secure area to the rear of a hatchback, with a screen to prevent them being thrown forward in the event of an accident.

89 'Red routes' in major cities have been introduced to

Mark one answer

- A. raise the speed limits
- B. help the traffic flow
- C. provide better parking
- D. allow lorries to load more freely

90 In some narrow residential streets you will find a speed limit of

Mark one answer

- A. 20mph
- B. 25mph
- C. 35mph
- D. 40mph

91 Road humps, chicanes, and narrowings are

Mark one answer

- A. always at major road works
- B. used to increase traffic speed
- C. at toll bridge approaches only
- D. traffic calming measures

92 The purpose of a catalytic converter is to reduce

Mark one answer

- A. fuel consumption
- B. the risk of fire
- C. toxic exhaust gases
- D. engine wear

93 Catalytic converters are fitted to make the

Mark one answer

- A. engine produce more power
- B. exhaust system easier to replace
- C. engine run quietly
- D. exhaust fumes cleaner

94 It is essential that tyre pressures are checked regularly. When should this be done?

Mark one answer

- A. After any lengthy journey
- B. After travelling at high speed
- C. When tyres are hot
- D. When tyres are cold

95 When should you NOT use your horn in a built-up area?

Mark one answer

- A. Between 8pm and 8am
- B. Between 9pm and dawn
- C. Between dusk and 8am
- D. Between 11.30pm and 7am

96 You will use more fuel if your tyres are

Mark one answer

- A. under-inflated
- B. of different makes
- C. over-inflated
- D. new and hardly used

97 How should you dispose of a used battery?

Mark two answers

- A. Take it to a local authority site
- B. Put it in the dustbin
- C. Break it up into pieces
- D. Leave it on waste land
- E. Take it to a garage
- F. Burn it on a fire

98 What is most likely to cause high fuel consumption?

Mark one answer

- A. Poor steering control
- B. Accelerating around bends
- C. Staying in high gears
- D. Harsh braking and accelerating

99 The fluid level in your battery is low. What should you top it up with?

Mark one answer

- A. Battery acid
- B. Distilled water
- C. Engine oil
- D. Engine coolant

100 You need top up your battery. What level should you fill to?

Mark one answer

- A. The top of the battery
- B. Half-way up the battery
- C. Just below the cell plates
- D. Just above the cell plates

101 You have too much oil in your engine. What could this cause?

Mark one answer

- A. Low oil pressure
- B. Engine overheating
- C. Chain wear
- D. Oil leaks

102 You are parking on a two-way road at night. The speed limit is 40mph. You should park on the

NI

Mark one answer

- A. left with parking lights on
- B. left with no lights on
- C. right with parking lights on
- D. right with dipped headlights on

103 You are parked on the road at night. Where must you use parking lights?

Mark one answer

- A. Where there are continuous white lines in the middle of the road
- B. Where the speed limit exceeds 30mph
- C. Where you are facing oncoming traffic
- D. Where you are near a bus stop

104 Which FOUR of these MUST be in good working order for your car to be roadworthy?

Mark four answers

- A. Temperature gauge
- B. Speedometer
- C. Windscreen washers
- D. Windscreen wiper
- E. Oil warning light
- F. Horn

105 New petrol-engined cars must be fitted with catalytic converters. The reason for this is to

Mark one answer

- A. control exhaust noise levels
- B. prolong the life of the exhaust system
- C. allow the exhaust system to be recycled
- D. reduce harmful exhaust emissions

106 What can cause heavy steering?

Mark one answer
- A. Driving on ice
- B. Badly worn brakes
- C. Over-inflated tyres
- D. Under-inflated tyres

107 Driving with under-inflated tyres can affect

Mark two answers
- A. engine temperature
- B. fuel consumption
- C. braking
- D. oil pressure

108 Excessive or uneven tyre wear can be caused by faults in the

Mark two answers
- A. gearbox
- B. braking system
- C. suspension
- D. exhaust system

109 The main cause of brake fade is

Mark one answer
- A. the brakes overheating
- B. air in the brake fluid
- C. oil on the brakes
- D. the brakes out of adjustment

110 Your anti-lock brakes warning light stays on. You should

Mark one answer
- A. check the brake fluid level
- B. check the footbrake free play
- C. check that the handbrake is released
- D. have the brakes checked immediately

111 What does this instrument panel light mean when lit?

Mark one answer
- A. Gear lever in park
- B. Gear lever in neutral
- C. Handbrake on
- D. Handbrake off

112 While driving, this warning light on your dashboard comes on. It means

Mark one answer
- A. a fault in the braking system
- B. the engine oil is low
- C. a rear light has failed
- D. your seat belt is not fastened

113 It is important to wear suitable shoes when you are driving. Why is this?

Mark one answer
- A. To prevent wear on the pedals
- B. To maintain control of the pedals
- C. To enable you to adjust your seat
- D. To enable you to walk for assistance if you break down

114 A properly adjusted head restraint will

Mark one answer
- A. make you more comfortable
- B. help you to avoid neck injury
- C. help you to relax
- D. help you to maintain your driving position

115 What will reduce the risk of neck injury resulting from a collision?

Mark one answer

- **A.** An air-sprung seat
- **B.** Anti-lock brakes
- **C.** A collapsible steering wheel
- **D.** A properly adjusted head restraint

116 You are driving a friend's children home from school. They are both under 14 years old. Who is responsible for making sure they wear a seat belt?

Mark one answer

- **A.** An adult passenger
- **B.** The children
- **C.** You, the driver
- **D.** Your friend

117 Car passengers MUST wear a seat belt if one is available, unless they are

Mark one answer

- **A.** under 14 years old
- **B.** under 1.5 metres (5 feet) in height
- **C.** sitting in the rear seat
- **D.** exempt for medical reasons

118 You are testing your suspension. You notice that your vehicle keeps bouncing when you press down on the front wing. What does this mean?

Mark one answer

- **A.** Worn tyres
- **B.** Tyres under-inflated
- **C.** Steering wheel not located centrally
- **D.** Worn shock absorbers

119 A roof rack fitted to your car will

Mark one answer

- **A.** reduce fuel consumption
- **B.** improve the road handling
- **C.** make your car go faster
- **D.** increase fuel consumption

120 It is illegal to drive with tyres that

Mark one answer

- **A.** have been bought second-hand
- **B.** have a large deep cut in the side wall
- **C.** are of different makes
- **D.** are of different tread patterns

121 The legal minimum depth of tread for car tyres over three quarters of the breadth is

Mark one answer

- **A.** 1mm
- **B.** 1.6mm
- **C.** 2.5mm
- **D.** 4mm

122 You are carrying two 13-year-old children and their parents in your car. Who is responsible for seeing that the children wear seat belts?

Mark one answer

- **A.** The children's parents
- **B.** You, the driver
- **C.** The front-seat passenger
- **D.** The children

123 When a roof rack is not in use it should be removed. Why is this?

Mark one answer

- A. It will affect the suspension
- B. It is illegal
- C. It will affect your braking
- D. It will waste fuel

124 You have a loose filler cap on your diesel fuel tank. This will

Mark two answers

- A. waste fuel and money
- B. make roads slippery for other road users
- C. improve your vehicle's fuel consumption
- D. increase the level of exhaust emissions

125 How can you, as a driver, help the environment?

Mark three answers

- A. By reducing your speed
- B. By gentle acceleration
- C. By using leaded fuel
- D. By driving faster
- E. By harsh acceleration
- F. By servicing your vehicle properly

126 To help the environment, you can avoid wasting fuel by

Mark three answers

- A. having your vehicle properly serviced
- B. making sure your tyres are correctly inflated
- C. not over-revving in the lower gears
- D. driving at higher speeds where possible
- E. keeping an empty roof rack properly fitted
- F. servicing your vehicle less regularly

127 To reduce the volume of traffic on the roads you could

Mark three answers

- A. use public transport more often
- B. share a car when possible
- C. walk or cycle on short journeys
- D. travel by car at all times
- E. use a car with a smaller engine
- F. drive in a bus lane

128 Which THREE of the following are most likely to waste fuel?

Mark three answers

- A. Reducing your speed
- B. Carrying unnecessary weight
- C. Using the wrong grade of fuel
- D. Under-inflated tyres
- E. Using different brands of fuel
- F. A fitted, empty roof rack

129 To avoid spillage after refuelling, you should make sure that

Mark one answer

- A. your tank is only ¾ full
- B. you have used a locking filler cap
- C. you check your fuel gauge is working
- D. your filler cap is securely fastened

130 Which THREE things can you, as a road user, do to help the environment?

Mark three answers

- A. Cycle when possible
- B. Drive on under-inflated tyres
- C. Use the choke for as long as possible on a cold engine
- D. Have your vehicle properly tuned and serviced
- E. Watch the traffic and plan ahead
- F. Brake as late as possible without skidding

131 As a driver you can cause MORE damage to the environment by

Mark three answers
- [ ] A. choosing a fuel-efficient vehicle
- [ ] B. making a lot of short journeys
- [ ] C. driving in as high a gear as possible
- [ ] D. accelerating as quickly as possible
- [ ] E. having your vehicle regularly serviced
- [ ] F. using leaded fuel

132 Extra care should be taken when refuelling, because diesel fuel when spilt is

Mark one answer
- [ ] A. sticky
- [ ] B. odourless
- [ ] C. clear
- [ ] D. slippery

133 To help protect the environment you should NOT

Mark one answer
- [ ] A. remove your roof rack when unloaded
- [ ] B. use your car for very short journeys
- [ ] C. walk, cycle, or use public transport
- [ ] D. empty the boot of unnecessary weight

134 Which THREE does the law require you to keep in good condition?

Mark three answers
- [ ] A. Gears
- [ ] B. Transmission
- [ ] C. Headlights
- [ ] D. Windscreen
- [ ] E. Seat belts

135 Driving at 70mph uses more fuel than driving at 50mph by up to

Mark one answer
- [ ] A. 10%
- [ ] B. 30%
- [ ] C. 75%
- [ ] D. 100%

136 Your vehicle pulls to one side when braking. You should

Mark one answer
- [ ] A. change the tyres around
- [ ] B. consult your garage as soon as possible
- [ ] C. pump the pedal when braking
- [ ] D. use your handbrake at the same time

137 As a driver you can help reduce pollution levels in town centres by

Mark one answer
- [ ] A. driving more quickly
- [ ] B. using leaded fuel
- [ ] C. walking or cycling
- [ ] D. driving short journeys

138 Unbalanced wheels on a car may cause

Mark one answer
- [ ] A. the steering to pull to one side
- [ ] B. the steering to vibrate
- [ ] C. the brakes to fail
- [ ] D. the tyres to deflate

139 Turning the steering wheel while your car is stationary can cause damage to the

Mark two answers
- [ ] A. gearbox
- [ ] B. engine
- [ ] C. brakes
- [ ] D. steering
- [ ] E. tyres

140 How can you reduce the chances of your car being broken into when leaving it unattended?

Mark one answer
- A. Take all contents with you
- B. Park near a taxi rank
- C. Place any valuables on the floor
- D. Park near a fire station

141 You have to leave valuables in your car. It would be safer to

Mark one answer
- A. put them in a carrier bag
- B. park near a school entrance
- C. lock them out of sight
- D. park near a bus stop

142 How could you deter theft from your car when leaving it unattended?

Mark one answer
- A. Leave valuables in a carrier bag
- B. Lock valuables out of sight
- C. Put valuables on the seats
- D. Leave valuables on the floor

143 Which of the following may help to deter a thief from stealing your car?

Mark one answer
- A. Always keeping the headlights on
- B. Fitting reflective glass windows
- C. Always keeping the interior light on
- D. Etching the car number on the windows

144 How can you help to prevent your car radio being stolen?

Mark one answer
- A. Park in an unlit area
- B. Hide the radio with a blanket
- C. Park near a busy junction
- D. Install a security coded radio

145 Which of the following should not be kept in your vehicle?

Mark one answer
- A. A first aid kit
- B. A road atlas
- C. The tax disc
- D. The vehicle documents

146 What should you do when leaving your vehicle?

Mark one answer
- A. Put valuable documents under the seats
- B. Remove all valuables
- C. Cover valuables with a blanket
- D. Leave the interior light on

147 You are parking your car. You have some valuables which you are unable to take with you. What should you do?

Mark one answer
- A. Park near a police station
- B. Put them under the driver's seat
- C. Lock them out of sight
- D. Park in an unlit side road

148 Which of these is most likely to deter the theft of your vehicle?

Mark one answer

- A. An immobiliser
- B. Tinted windows
- C. Locking wheel nuts
- D. A sun screen

149 Wherever possible, which one of the following should you do when parking at night?

Mark one answer

- A. Park in a quiet car park
- B. Park in a well-lit area
- C. Park facing against the flow of traffic
- D. Park next to a busy junction

150 When parking and leaving your car you should

Mark one answer

- A. park under a shady tree
- B. remove the tax disc
- C. park in a quiet road
- D. engage the steering lock

151 Rear facing baby seats should NEVER be used on a seat protected with

Mark one answer

- A. an airbag
- B. seat belts
- C. head restraints
- D. seat covers

152 When leaving your vehicle parked and unattended you should

Mark one answer

- A. park near a busy junction
- B. park in a housing estate
- C. remove the key and lock it
- D. leave the left indicator on

153 How can you lessen the risk of your vehicle being broken into at night?

Mark one answer

- A. Leave it in a well-lit area
- B. Park in a quiet side road
- C. Don't engage the steering lock
- D. Park in a poorly lit area

154 To help keep your car secure you could join a

Mark one answer

- A. vehicle breakdown organisation
- B. vehicle watch scheme
- C. advanced drivers scheme
- D. car maintenance class

155 Which TWO of the following will improve fuel consumption?

Mark two answers

- A. Reducing your road speed
- B. Planning well ahead
- C. Late and harsh braking
- D. Driving in lower gears
- E. Short journeys with a cold engine
- F. Rapid acceleration

156 You service your own vehicle. How should you get rid of the old engine oil?

Mark one answer

- **A.** Take it to a local authority site
- **B.** Pour it down a drain
- **C.** Tip it into a hole in the ground
- **D.** Put it into your dustbin

157 On your vehicle, where would you find a catalytic converter?

Mark one answer

- **A.** In the fuel tank
- **B.** In the air filter
- **C.** On the cooling system
- **D.** On the exhaust system

158 Why do MOT tests include a strict exhaust emission test?

Mark one answer

- **A.** To recover the cost of expensive garage equipment
- **B.** To help protect the environment against pollution
- **C.** To discover which fuel supplier is used the most
- **D.** To make sure diesel and petrol engines emit the same fumes

159 To reduce the damage your vehicle causes to the environment you should

Mark three answers

- **A.** use narrow side streets
- **B.** avoid harsh acceleration
- **C.** brake in good time
- **D.** anticipate well ahead
- **E.** use busy routes

160 Your vehicle has a catalytic converter. Its purpose is to reduce

Mark one answer

- **A.** exhaust noise
- **B.** fuel consumption
- **C.** exhaust emissions
- **D.** engine noise

161 A properly serviced vehicle will give

Mark two answers

- **A.** lower insurance premiums
- **B.** you a refund on your road tax
- **C.** better fuel economy
- **D.** cleaner exhaust emissions

162 You enter a road where there are road humps. What should you do?

Mark one answer

- **A.** Maintain a reduced speed throughout
- **B.** Accelerate quickly between each one
- **C.** Always keep to the maximum legal speed
- **D.** Drive slowly at school times only

TIP Do not drive with an empty roof rack on your car. By increasing drag, the roof rack can eat up more than 10% of your total fuel consumption.

163 When should you especially check the engine oil level?

Mark one answer

- [ ] **A.** Before a long journey
- [ ] **B.** When the engine is hot
- [ ] **C.** Early in the morning
- [ ] **D.** Every 6,000 miles

164 You are having difficulty finding a parking space in a busy town. You can see there is space on the zigzag lines of a zebra crossing. Can you park there?

Mark one answer

- [ ] **A.** No, unless you stay with your car
- [ ] **B.** Yes, in order to drop off a passenger
- [ ] **C.** Yes, if you do not block people from crossing
- [ ] **D.** No, not in any circumstances

165 When leaving your car unattended for a few minutes you should

Mark one answer

- [ ] **A.** leave the engine running
- [ ] **B.** switch the engine off but leave the key in
- [ ] **C.** lock it and remove the key
- [ ] **D.** park near a traffic warden

166 When parking and leaving your car for a few minutes you should

Mark one answer

- [ ] **A.** leave it unlocked
- [ ] **B.** lock it and remove the key
- [ ] **C.** leave the hazard warning lights on
- [ ] **D.** leave the interior light on

167 When leaving your car to help keep it secure you should

Mark one answer

- [ ] **A.** leave the hazard warning lights on
- [ ] **B.** lock it and remove the key
- [ ] **C.** park on a one-way street
- [ ] **D.** park in a residential area

168 When leaving your vehicle where should you park if possible?

Mark one answer

- [ ] **A.** Opposite a traffic island
- [ ] **B.** In a secure car park
- [ ] **C.** On a bend
- [ ] **D.** At or near a taxi rank

169 You are leaving your vehicle parked on a road. When may you leave the engine running?

Mark one answer

- [ ] **A.** If you will be parking for less than five minutes
- [ ] **B.** If the battery is flat
- [ ] **C.** When in a 20mph zone
- [ ] **D.** Never on any occasion

TIP If you have a petrol-fuelled car built after 1992, it will be fitted with a **catalytic converter**. *Catalyst* means something that enables a chemical change to take place; the catalytic converter, which is located in the car's exhaust system, converts pollutant gases into less harmful gases.

170

In which THREE places would parking your vehicle cause danger or obstruction to other road users?

Mark three answers

- [ ] **A.** In front of a property entrance
- [ ] **B.** At or near a bus stop
- [ ] **C.** On your driveway
- [ ] **D.** In a marked parking space
- [ ] **E.** On the approach to a level crossing

TIP Driving a four-wheel drive vehicle (4WD) demands different techniques; a 4WD has a higher centre of gravity, and is more likely to topple over if you are forced to swerve or drive too fast around a tight corner. The advantage of 4WD is that it has better road holding capabilities and is excellent over rough terrain.

171

In which THREE places would parking cause an obstruction to others?

Mark three answers

- [ ] **A.** Near the brow of a hill
- [ ] **B.** In a lay-by
- [ ] **C.** Where the kerb is raised
- [ ] **D.** Where the kerb has been lowered for wheelchairs
- [ ] **E.** At or near a bus stop

172

You are away from home and have to park your vehicle overnight. Where should you leave it?

Mark one answer

- [ ] **A.** Opposite another parked vehicle
- [ ] **B.** In a quiet road
- [ ] **C.** Opposite a traffic island
- [ ] **D.** In a secure car park

173 Braking distances on ice can be

Mark one answer

- [ ] **A.** twice the normal distance
- [ ] **B.** five times the normal distance
- [ ] **C.** seven times the normal distance
- [ ] **D.** ten times the normal distance

174 Freezing conditions will affect the distance it takes you to come to a stop. You should expect stopping distances to increase by up to

Mark one answer

- [ ] **A.** two times
- [ ] **B.** three times
- [ ] **C.** five times
- [ ] **D.** ten times

175 In very hot weather the road surface can get soft. Which TWO of the following will be affected most?

Mark two answers

- [ ] **A.** The suspension
- [ ] **B.** The grip of the tyres
- [ ] **C.** The braking
- [ ] **D.** The exhaust

176 Where are you most likely to be affected by a side wind?

Mark one answer

- [ ] **A.** On a narrow country lane
- [ ] **B.** On an open stretch of road
- [ ] **C.** On a busy stretch of road
- [ ] **D.** On a long, straight road

177 In windy conditions you need to take extra care when

Mark one answer

- [ ] **A.** using the brakes
- [ ] **B.** making a hill start
- [ ] **C.** turning into a narrow road
- [ ] **D.** passing pedal cyclists

178 What is the shortest stopping distance at 70mph?

Mark one answer

- [ ] **A.** 53 metres (175 feet)
- [ ] **B.** 60 metres (197 feet)
- [ ] **C.** 73 metres (240 feet)
- [ ] **D.** 96 metres (315 feet)

179 What is the shortest overall stopping distance on a dry road from 60mph?

Mark one answer

- [ ] **A.** 53 metres (175 feet)
- [ ] **B.** 58 metres (190 feet)
- [ ] **C.** 73 metres (240 feet)
- [ ] **D.** 96 metres (315 feet)

180 Your indicators may be difficult to see in bright sunlight. What should you do?

Mark one answer

- [ ] **A.** Put your indicator on earlier
- [ ] **B.** Give an arm signal as well as using your indicator
- [ ] **C.** Touch the brake several times to show the stop lights
- [ ] **D.** Turn as quickly as you can

181 In very hot weather the road surface can get soft. Which TWO of the following will be affected most?

Mark two answers
- [ ] **A.** The suspension
- [ ] **B.** The steering
- [ ] **C.** The braking
- [ ] **D.** The exhaust

182 When approaching a right-hand bend you should keep well to the left. Why is this?

Mark one answer
- [ ] **A.** To improve your view of the road
- [ ] **B.** To overcome the effect of the road's slope
- [ ] **C.** To let faster traffic from behind overtake
- [ ] **D.** To be positioned safely if you skid

183 You should not overtake when

Mark three answers
- [ ] **A.** intending to turn left shortly afterwards
- [ ] **B.** in a one-way street
- [ ] **C.** approaching a junction
- [ ] **D.** going up a long hill
- [ ] **E.** the view ahead is blocked

TIP Don't forget – you may have to deal with more than one hazard at a time!

184 You have just gone through deep water. To dry off the brakes you should

Mark one answer
- [ ] **A.** accelerate and keep to a high speed for a short time
- [ ] **B.** go slowly while gently applying the brakes
- [ ] **C.** avoid using the brakes at all for a few miles
- [ ] **D.** stop for at least an hour to allow them time to dry

185 You are on a fast, open road in good conditions. For safety, the distance between you and the vehicle in front should be

Mark one answer
- [ ] **A.** a two-second time gap
- [ ] **B.** one car length
- [ ] **C.** 2 metres (6 feet 6 inches)
- [ ] **D.** two-car lengths

186 What is the most common cause of skidding?

Mark one answer
- [ ] **A.** Worn tyres
- [ ] **B.** Driver error
- [ ] **C.** Other vehicles
- [ ] **D.** Pedestrians

187 You are driving on an icy road. How can you avoid wheelspin?

Mark one answer
- [ ] **A.** Drive at a slow speed in as high a gear as possible
- [ ] **B.** Use the handbrake if the wheels start to slip
- [ ] **C.** Brake gently and repeatedly
- [ ] **D.** Drive in a low gear at all times

188 Skidding is mainly caused by

Mark one answer
- A. the weather
- B. the driver
- C. the vehicle
- D. the road

189 You are driving in freezing conditions. What should you do when approaching a sharp bend?

Mark two answers
- A. Slow down before you reach the bend
- B. Gently apply your handbrake
- C. Firmly use your footbrake
- D. Coast into the bend
- E. Avoid sudden steering movements

190 You are turning left on a slippery road. The back of your vehicle slides to the right. You should

Mark one answer
- A. brake firmly and not turn the steering wheel
- B. steer carefully to the left
- C. steer carefully to the right
- D. brake firmly and steer to the left

191 You are braking on a wet road. Your vehicle begins to skid. Your vehicle does not have anti-lock brakes. What is the FIRST thing you should do?

Mark one answer
- A. Quickly pull up the handbrake
- B. Release the footbrake fully
- C. Push harder on the brake pedal
- D. Gently use the accelerator

192 Coasting the vehicle

Mark one answer
- A. improves the driver's control
- B. makes steering easier
- C. reduces the driver's control
- D. uses more fuel

193 Before starting a journey in freezing weather you should clear ice and snow from your vehicle's

Mark four answers
- A. aerial
- B. windows
- C. bumper
- D. lights
- E. mirrors
- F. number plates

194 You are trying to move off on snow. You should use

Mark one answer
- A. the lowest gear you can
- B. the highest gear you can
- C. a high engine speed
- D. the handbrake and footbrake together

195 When driving in falling snow you should

Mark one answer
- A. brake firmly and quickly
- B. be ready to steer sharply
- C. use sidelights only
- D. brake gently in plenty of time

196
The MAIN benefit of having four-wheel drive is to improve

Mark one answer

- A. road holding
- B. fuel consumption
- C. stopping distances
- D. passenger comfort

197
You are about to go down a steep hill. To control the speed of your vehicle you should

Mark one answer

- A. select a high gear and use the brakes carefully
- B. select a high gear and use the brakes firmly
- C. select a low gear and use the brakes carefully
- D. select a low gear and avoid using the brakes

198
How can you use the engine of your vehicle as a brake?

Mark one answer

- A. By changing to a lower gear
- B. By selecting reverse gear
- C. By changing to a higher gear
- D. By selecting neutral gear

199
You wish to park facing DOWNHILL. Which TWO of the following should you do?

Mark two answers

- A. Turn the steering wheel towards the kerb
- B. Park close to the bumper of another car
- C. Park with two wheels on the kerb
- D. Put the handbrake on firmly
- E. Turn the steering wheel away from the kerb

200
You are driving in a built-up area. You approach a speed hump. You should

Mark one answer

- A. move across to the left-hand side of the road
- B. wait for any pedestrians to cross
- C. slow your vehicle right down
- D. stop and check both pavements

201
You are on a long, downhill slope. What should you do to help control the speed of your vehicle?

Mark one answer

- A. Select neutral
- B. Select a lower gear
- C. Grip the handbrake firmly
- D. Apply the parking brake gently

202
Your vehicle is fitted with anti-lock brakes. To stop quickly in an emergency you should

Mark one answer   **NI**

- A. brake firmly and pump the brake pedal on and off
- B. brake rapidly and firmly without releasing the brake pedal
- C. brake gently and pump the brake pedal on and off
- D. brake rapidly once, and immediately release the brake pedal

203 Anti-lock brakes prevent wheels from locking. This means the tyres are less likely to

Mark one answer

- A. aquaplane
- B. skid
- C. puncture
- D. wear

204 Anti-lock brakes reduce the chances of a skid occurring particularly when

Mark one answer

- A. driving down steep hills
- B. braking during normal driving
- C. braking in an emergency
- D. driving on good road surfaces

205 Anti-lock brakes are most effective when you

Mark one answer **NI**

- A. keep pumping the footbrake to prevent skidding
- B. brake normally, but grip the steering wheel tightly
- C. brake rapidly and firmly until you have slowed down
- D. apply the handbrake to reduce the stopping distance

206 Your car is fitted with anti-lock brakes. You need to stop in an emergency. You should

Mark one answer **NI**

- A. brake normally and avoid turning the steering wheel
- B. press the brake pedal rapidly and firmly until you have stopped
- C. keep pushing and releasing the footbrake quickly to prevent skidding
- D. apply the handbrake to reduce the stopping distance

207 Vehicles fitted with anti-lock brakes

Mark one answer

- A. are impossible to skid
- B. can be steered while you are braking
- C. accelerate much faster
- D. are not fitted with a handbrake

208 Anti-lock brakes may not work as effectively if the road surface is

Mark two answers

- A. dry
- B. loose
- C. wet
- D. good
- E. firm

209 Anti-lock brakes are of most use when you are

Mark one answer

- A. braking gently
- B. driving on worn tyres
- C. braking excessively
- D. driving normally

210 Driving a vehicle fitted with anti-lock brakes allows you to

Mark one answer

- A. brake harder because it is impossible to skid
- B. drive at higher speeds
- C. steer and brake at the same time
- D. pay less attention to the road ahead

211 Anti-lock brakes can greatly assist with

Mark one answer

- A. a higher cruising speed
- B. steering control when braking
- C. control when accelerating
- D. motorway driving

212 When would an anti-lock braking system start to work?

Mark one answer

- A. After the parking brake has been applied
- B. Whenever pressure on the brake pedal is applied
- C. Just as the wheels are about to lock
- D. When the normal braking system fails to operate

213 You are driving a vehicle fitted with anti-lock brakes. You need to stop in an emergency. You should apply the footbrake

NI

Mark one answer

- A. slowly and gently
- B. slowly but firmly
- C. rapidly and gently
- D. rapidly and firmly

214 Your vehicle has anti-lock brakes, but they may not always prevent skidding. This is most likely to happen when driving

Mark two answers

- A. in foggy conditions
- B. on surface water
- C. on loose road surfaces
- D. on dry tarmac
- E. at night on unlit roads

215 Anti-lock brakes will take effect when

Mark one answer

- A. you do not brake quickly enough
- B. excessive brake pressure has been applied
- C. you have not seen a hazard ahead
- D. speeding on slippery road surfaces

216 When driving in fog, which of the following are correct?

Mark three answers

- A. Use dipped headlights
- B. Use headlights on full beam
- C. Allow more time for your journey
- D. Keep close to the car in front
- E. Slow down
- F. Use sidelights only

TIP Never coast downhill. Keep in a low gear so that you have engine braking as well as the footbrake. The lower the gear the stronger the engine braking.

217

You are driving along a country road. You see this sign. AFTER dealing safely with the hazard you should always

Mark one answer

- **A.** check your tyre pressures
- **B.** switch on your hazard warning lights
- **C.** accelerate briskly
- **D.** test your brakes

218

You are driving in heavy rain. Your steering suddenly becomes very light. You should

Mark one answer

- **A.** steer towards the side of the road
- **B.** apply gentle acceleration
- **C.** brake firmly to reduce speed
- **D.** ease off the accelerator

219

How can you tell when you are driving over black ice?

Mark one answer

- **A.** It is easier to brake
- **B.** The noise from your tyres sounds louder
- **C.** You see black ice on the road
- **D.** Your steering feels light

220

The roads are icy. You should drive slowly

Mark one answer

- **A.** in the highest gear possible
- **B.** in the lowest gear possible
- **C.** with the handbrake partly on
- **D.** with your left foot on the brake

221

You are driving along a wet road. How can you tell if your vehicle is aquaplaning?

Mark one answer

- **A.** The engine will stall
- **B.** The engine noise will increase
- **C.** The steering will feel very heavy
- **D.** The steering will feel very light

222

How can you tell if you are driving on ice?

Mark two answers

- **A.** The tyres make a rumbling noise
- **B.** The tyres make hardly any noise
- **C.** The steering becomes heavier
- **D.** The steering becomes lighter

223

You are driving along a wet road. How can you tell if your vehicle's tyres are losing their grip on the surface?

Mark one answer

- **A.** The engine will stall
- **B.** The steering will feel very heavy
- **C.** The engine noise will increase
- **D.** The steering will feel very light

224 You are travelling at 50mph on a good, dry road. What is your shortest overall stopping distance?

Mark one answer

- **A.** 36 metres (120 feet)
- **B.** 53 metres (175 feet)
- **C.** 75 metres (245 feet)
- **D.** 96 metres (315 feet)

225 Your overall stopping distance will be much longer when driving

Mark one answer

- **A.** in the rain
- **B.** in fog
- **C.** at night
- **D.** in strong winds

226 You have driven through a flood. What is the first thing you should do?

Mark one answer

- **A.** Stop and check the tyres
- **B.** Stop and dry the brakes
- **C.** Check your exhaust
- **D.** Test your brakes

227 You are on a good, dry road surface. Your vehicle has good brakes and tyres. What is the BRAKING distance at 50mph?

Mark one answer

- **A.** 38 metres (125 feet)
- **B.** 14 metres (46 feet)
- **C.** 24 metres (79 feet)
- **D.** 55 metres (180 feet)

228 You are on a good, dry, road surface and your vehicle has good brakes and tyres. What is the typical overall stopping distance at 40mph?

Mark one answer

- **A.** 23 metres (75 feet)
- **B.** 36 metres (120 feet)
- **C.** 53 metres (175 feet)
- **D.** 96 metres (315 feet)

TIP Remember the 'two-second rule'? Well you can 'Say it again when driving in rain!' In other words, you need to allow at least twice the distance for braking and stopping in wet weather.

229

You see this sign on the rear of a slow-moving lorry that you want to pass. It is travelling in the middle lane of a three-lane motorway. You should

Mark one answer

- **A.** cautiously approach the lorry then pass on either side
- **B.** follow the lorry until you can leave the motorway
- **C.** wait on the hard shoulder until the lorry has stopped
- **D.** approach with care and keep to the left of the lorry

230

Where would you expect to see these markers?

Mark two answers

- **A.** On a motorway sign
- **B.** At the entrance to a narrow bridge
- **C.** On a large goods vehicle
- **D.** On a builder's skip placed on the road

231

What does this signal from a police officer, mean to oncoming traffic?

Mark one answer

- **A.** Go ahead
- **B.** Stop
- **C.** Turn left
- **D.** Turn right

232

What is the main hazard shown in this picture?

Mark one answer

- **A.** Vehicles turning right
- **B.** Vehicles doing U-turns
- **C.** The cyclist crossing the road
- **D.** Parked cars around the corner

233 Which road user has caused a hazard?

Mark one answer
- **A.** The parked car (arrowed A)
- **B.** The pedestrian waiting to cross (arrowed B)
- **C.** The moving car (arrowed C)
- **D.** The car turning (arrowed D)

234 What should the driver of the car approaching the crossing do?

Mark one answer
- **A.** Continue at the same speed
- **B.** Sound the horn
- **C.** Drive through quickly
- **D.** Slow down and get ready to stop

235 What THREE things should the driver of the grey car (arrowed) be especially aware of?

Mark three answers
- **A.** Pedestrians stepping out between cars
- **B.** Other cars behind the grey car
- **C.** Doors opening on parked cars
- **D.** The bumpy road surface
- **E.** Cars leaving parking spaces
- **F.** Empty parking spaces

236 You think the driver of the vehicle in front has forgotten to cancel the right indicator. You should

Mark one answer
- **A.** flash your lights to alert the driver
- **B.** sound your horn before overtaking
- **C.** overtake on the left if there is room
- **D.** stay behind and not overtake

> **TIP** If you are driving past parked cars, it is a good idea to leave as much space as the width of a car door – in case one opens suddenly. If you can't give that much space, slow down so that you could **stop** if necessary.

237
What is the main hazard the driver of the red car (arrowed) should be most aware of?

Mark one answer

- [ ] **A.** Glare from the sun may affect the driver's vision
- [ ] **B.** The black car may stop suddenly
- [ ] **C.** The bus may move out into the road
- [ ] **D.** Oncoming vehicles will assume the driver is turning right

238
In heavy motorway traffic you are being followed closely by the vehicle behind. How can you lower the risk of an accident?

Mark one answer

- [ ] **A.** Increase your distance from the vehicle in front
- [ ] **B.** Tap your foot on the brake pedal sharply
- [ ] **C.** Switch on your hazard lights
- [ ] **D.** Move on to the hard shoulder and stop

239
You see this sign ahead. You should expect the road to

Mark one answer

- [ ] **A.** go steeply uphill
- [ ] **B.** go steeply downhill
- [ ] **C.** bend sharply to the left
- [ ] **D.** bend sharply to the right

240
You are approaching this cyclist. You should

Mark one answer

- [ ] **A.** overtake before the cyclist gets to the junction
- [ ] **B.** flash your headlights at the cyclist
- [ ] **C.** slow down and allow the cyclist to turn
- [ ] **D.** overtake the cyclist on the left-hand side

241 Why must you take extra care when turning right at this junction?

Mark one answer
- **A.** Road surface is poor
- **B.** Footpaths are narrow
- **C.** Road markings are faint
- **D.** There is reduced visibility

242 This yellow sign on a vehicle indicates this is

Mark one answer
- **A.** a vehicle broken down
- **B.** a school bus
- **C.** an ice-cream van
- **D.** a private ambulance

243 When approaching this bridge you should give way to

Mark one answer
- **A.** bicycles
- **B.** buses
- **C.** motorcycles
- **D.** cars

244 What type of vehicle could you expect to meet in the middle of the road?

Mark one answer
- **A.** Lorry
- **B.** Bicycle
- **C.** Car
- **D.** Motorcycle

> **TIP** Driver sleepiness is thought to cause at least 10% of all road accidents and one in five of accidents on motorways and major roads.

245 At this blind junction you must stop

Mark one answer

- [ ] **A.** behind the line, then edge forward to see clearly
- [ ] **B.** beyond the line at a point where you can see clearly
- [ ] **C.** only if there is traffic on the main road
- [ ] **D.** only if you are turning to the right

246 A driver pulls out of a side road in front of you. You have to brake hard. You should

Mark one answer

- [ ] **A.** ignore the error and stay calm
- [ ] **B.** flash your lights to show your annoyance
- [ ] **C.** sound your horn to show your annoyance
- [ ] **D.** overtake as soon as possible

247 An elderly person's driving ability could be affected because they may be unable to

Mark one answer

- [ ] **A.** obtain car insurance
- [ ] **B.** understand road signs
- [ ] **C.** react very quickly
- [ ] **D.** give signals correctly

248 You have just passed these warning lights. What hazard would you expect to see next?

Mark one answer

- [ ] **A.** A level crossing with no barrier
- [ ] **B.** An ambulance station
- [ ] **C.** A school crossing patrol
- [ ] **D.** An opening bridge

249 Why should you be especially cautious when going past this bus?

Mark two answers

- [ ] **A.** There is traffic approaching in the distance
- [ ] **B.** The driver may open the door
- [ ] **C.** It may suddenly move off
- [ ] **D.** People may cross the road in front of it
- [ ] **E.** There are bicycles parked on the pavement

250 In areas where there are 'traffic calming' measures you should

Mark one answer

- [ ] **A.** drive at a reduced speed
- [ ] **B.** always drive at the speed limit
- [ ] **C.** position in the centre of the road
- [ ] **D.** only slow down if pedestrians are near

251 You are planning a long journey. Do you need to plan rest stops?

Mark one answer

- **A.** Yes, you should plan to stop every half an hour
- **B.** Yes, regular stops help concentration
- **C.** No, you will be less tired if you get there as soon as possible
- **D.** No, only fuel stops will be needed

252 A driver does something that upsets you. You should

Mark one answer

- **A.** try not to react
- **B.** let them know how you feel
- **C.** flash your headlights several times
- **D.** sound your horn

253 The red lights are flashing. What should you do when approaching this level crossing?

Mark one answer

- **A.** Go through quickly
- **B.** Go through carefully
- **C.** Stop before the barrier
- **D.** Switch on hazard warning lights

254 What are TWO main hazards you should be aware of when going along this street?

Mark two answers

- **A.** Glare from the sun
- **B.** Car doors opening suddenly
- **C.** Lack of road markings
- **D.** The headlights on parked cars being switched on
- **E.** Large goods vehicles
- **F.** Children running out from between vehicles

255 What is the main hazard you should be aware of when following this cyclist?

Mark one answer

- **A.** The cyclist may move into the left and dismount
- **B.** The cyclist may swerve out into the road
- **C.** The contents of the cyclist's carrier may fall on to the road
- **D.** The cyclist may wish to turn right at the end of the road

256 When approaching this hazard why should you slow down?

Mark two answers

- A. Because of the bend
- B. Because it's hard to see to the right
- C. Because of approaching traffic
- D. Because of animals crossing
- E. Because of the level crossing

257 A driver's behaviour has upset you. It may help if you

Mark one answer

- A. stop and take a break
- B. shout abusive language
- C. gesture to them with your hand
- D. follow their car, flashing the headlights

258 You are on a dual carriageway. Ahead you see a vehicle with an amber flashing light. What will this be?

Mark one answer

- A. An ambulance
- B. A fire engine
- C. A doctor on call
- D. A disabled person's vehicle

259 You are approaching crossroads. The traffic lights have failed. What should you do?

Mark one answer

- A. Brake and stop only for large vehicles
- B. Brake sharply to a stop before looking
- C. Be prepared to brake sharply to a stop
- D. Be prepared to stop for any traffic.

260 Why are destination markings painted on the road surface?

Mark one answer

- A. To restrict the flow of traffic
- B. To warn you of oncoming traffic
- C. To enable you to change lanes early
- D. To prevent you changing lanes

261 What should the driver of the red car (arrowed) do?

Mark one answer

- A. Wave the pedestrians who are waiting to cross
- B. Wait for the pedestrian in the road to cross
- C. Quickly drive behind the pedestrian in the road
- D. Tell the pedestrian in the road she should not have crossed

262
You are following a slower-moving vehicle on a narrow country road. There is a junction just ahead on the right. What should you do?

Mark one answer

- [ ] **A.** Overtake after checking your mirrors and signalling
- [ ] **B.** Stay behind until you are past the junction
- [ ] **C.** Accelerate quickly to pass before the junction
- [ ] **D.** Slow down and prepare to overtake on the left

263
What should you do as you approach this overhead bridge?

Mark one answer

- [ ] **A.** Move out to the centre of the road before going through
- [ ] **B.** Find another route, this is only for high vehicles
- [ ] **C.** Be prepared to give way to large vehicles in the middle of the road
- [ ] **D.** Move across to the right-hand side before going through

264
Why are mirrors often slightly curved (convex)?

Mark one answer

- [ ] **A.** They give a wider field of vision
- [ ] **B.** They totally cover blind spots
- [ ] **C.** They make it easier to judge the speed of following traffic
- [ ] **D.** They make following traffic look bigger

265
What does the solid white line at the side of the road indicate?

Mark one answer

- [ ] **A.** Traffic lights ahead
- [ ] **B.** Edge of the carriageway
- [ ] **C.** Footpath on the left
- [ ] **D.** Cycle path

266
You are driving towards this level crossing. What would be the first warning of an approaching train?

Mark one answer

- [ ] **A.** Both half-barriers down
- [ ] **B.** A steady amber light
- [ ] **C.** One half-barrier down
- [ ] **D.** Twin flashing red lights

TIP Leave sufficient room to allow for the mistakes of others. After all, if an accident occurs, the fact that it was not your fault will be little consolation.

267

You are driving along this motorway. It is raining. When following this lorry you should

Mark two answers

- **A.** allow at least a two-second gap
- **B.** move left and drive on the hard shoulder
- **C.** allow at least a four-second gap
- **D.** be aware of spray reducing your vision
- **E.** move right and stay in the right-hand lane

268

You are behind this cyclist. When the traffic lights change, what should you do?

Mark one answer

- **A.** Try to move off before the cyclist
- **B.** Allow the cyclist time and room
- **C.** Turn right but give the cyclist room
- **D.** Tap your horn and drive through first

269

You are driving towards this left-hand bend. What dangers should you be aware of?

Mark one answer

- **A.** A vehicle overtaking you
- **B.** No white lines in the centre of the road
- **C.** No sign to warn you of the bend
- **D.** Pedestrians walking towards you

270

While driving, you see this sign ahead. You should

Mark one answer

- **A.** stop at the sign
- **B.** slow, but continue around the bend
- **C.** slow to a crawl and continue
- **D.** stop and look for open farm gates

271 Why should the junction on the left be kept clear?

Mark one answer

- [ ] **A.** To allow vehicles to enter and emerge
- [ ] **B.** To allow the bus to reverse
- [ ] **C.** To allow vehicles to make a U-turn
- [ ] **D.** To allow vehicles to park

272 When the traffic lights change to green the white car should

Mark one answer

- [ ] **A.** wait for the cyclist to pull away
- [ ] **B.** move off quickly and turn in front of the cyclist
- [ ] **C.** move close up to the cyclist to beat the lights
- [ ] **D.** sound the horn to warn the cyclist

273 You intend to turn left at the traffic lights. Just before turning you should

Mark one answer

- [ ] **A.** check your right mirror
- [ ] **B.** move close up to the white car
- [ ] **C.** straddle the lanes
- [ ] **D.** check for bicycles on your left

274 You should reduce your speed when driving along this road because

Mark one answer

- [ ] **A.** there is a staggered junction ahead
- [ ] **B.** there is a low bridge ahead
- [ ] **C.** there is a change in the road surface
- [ ] **D.** the road ahead narrows

275 You are driving at 60mph. As you approach this hazard you should

Mark one answer

- [ ] **A.** maintain your speed
- [ ] **B.** reduce your speed
- [ ] **C.** take the next right turn
- [ ] **D.** take the next left turn

276 The traffic ahead of you in the left lane is slowing. You should

Mark two answers

- [ ] **A.** be wary of cars on your right cutting in
- [ ] **B.** accelerate past the vehicles in the left lane
- [ ] **C.** pull up on the left-hand verge
- [ ] **D.** move across and continue in the right-hand lane
- [ ] **E.** slow down keeping a safe separation distance

277 What might you expect to happen in this situation?

Mark one answer

- [ ] **A.** Traffic will move into the right-hand lane
- [ ] **B.** Traffic speed will increase
- [ ] **C.** Traffic will move into the left-hand lane
- [ ] **D.** Traffic will not need to change position

278 You are driving on a road with several lanes. You see these signs above the lanes. What do they mean?

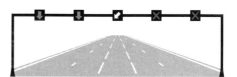

Mark one answer

- [ ] **A.** The two right lanes are open
- [ ] **B.** The two left lanes are open
- [ ] **C.** Traffic in the left lanes should stop
- [ ] **D.** Traffic in the right lanes should stop

279 As a provisional licence holder, you must not drive a motor car

Mark two answers **NI**

- A. at more than 50mph
- B. on your own
- C. on the motorway
- D. under the age of 18 years of age at night
- E. with passengers in the rear seats

280 After passing your driving test, you suffer from ill health. This affects your driving. You MUST

Mark one answer

- A. inform your local police station
- B. get on as best you can
- C. not inform anyone as you hold a full licence
- D. inform the licensing authority

281 You are invited to a pub lunch. You know that you will have to drive in the evening. What is your best course of action?

Mark one answer

- A. Avoid mixing your alcoholic drinks
- B. Not drink any alcohol at all
- C. Have some milk before drinking alcohol
- D. Eat a hot meal with your alcoholic drinks

282 You have been convicted of driving whilst unfit through drink or drugs. You will find this is likely to cause the cost of one of the following to rise considerably. Which one?

Mark one answer

- A. Road fund licence
- B. Insurance premiums
- C. Vehicle test certificate
- D. Driving licence

283 What advice should you give to a driver who has had a few alcoholic drinks at a party?

Mark one answer

- A. Have a strong cup of coffee and then drive home
- B. Drive home carefully and slowly
- C. Go home by public transport
- D. Wait a short while and then drive home

284 You have been taking medicine for a few days which made you feel drowsy. Today you feel better but still need to take the medicine. You should only drive

Mark one answer

- A. if your journey is necessary
- B. at night on quiet roads
- C. if someone goes with you
- D. after checking with your doctor

285
You are about to return home from holiday when you become ill. A doctor prescribes drugs which are likely to affect your driving. You should

Mark one answer

- A. drive only if someone is with you
- B. avoid driving on motorways
- C. not drive yourself
- D. never drive at more than 30mph

286
During periods of illness your ability to drive may be impaired. You MUST

Mark two answers

- A. see your doctor each time before you drive
- B. only take smaller doses of any medicines
- C. be medically fit to drive
- D. not drive after taking certain medicines
- E. take all your medicines with you when you drive

287
You feel drowsy when driving. You should

Mark two answers

- A. stop and rest as soon as possible
- B. turn the heater up to keep you warm and comfortable
- C. make sure you have a good supply of fresh air
- D. continue with your journey but drive more slowly
- E. close the car windows to help you concentrate

288
You are driving along a motorway and become tired. You should

Mark two answers

- A. stop at the next service area and rest
- B. leave the motorway at the next exit and rest
- C. increase your speed and turn up the radio volume
- D. close all your windows and set heating to warm
- E. pull up on the hard shoulder and change drivers

289
You are taking drugs that are likely to affect your driving. What should you do?

Mark one answer

- A. Seek medical advice before driving
- B. Limit your driving to essential journeys
- C. Only drive if accompanied by a full licence-holder
- D. Drive only for short distances

290
You are about to drive home. You feel very tired and have a severe headache. You should

Mark one answer

- A. wait until you are fit and well before driving
- B. drive home, but take a tablet for headaches
- C. drive home if you can stay awake for the journey
- D. wait for a short time, then drive home slowly

291 If you are feeling tired it is best to stop as soon as you can. Until then you should

Mark one answer

- [ ] A. increase your speed to find a stopping place quickly
- [ ] B. ensure a supply of fresh air
- [ ] C. gently tap the steering wheel
- [ ] D. keep changing speed to improve concentration

292 If your motorway journey seems boring and you feel drowsy whilst driving you should

Mark one answer

- [ ] A. open a window and drive to the next service area
- [ ] B. stop on the hard shoulder for a sleep
- [ ] C. speed up to arrive at your destination sooner
- [ ] D. slow down and let other drivers overtake

293 Driving long distances can be tiring. You can prevent this by

Mark three answers

- [ ] A. stopping every so often for a walk
- [ ] B. opening a window for some fresh air
- [ ] C. ensuring plenty of refreshment breaks
- [ ] D. completing the journey without stopping
- [ ] E. eating a large meal before driving

TIP The reason motorcyclists have their headlamps on in daylight is to make them more visible to other road users.

294 You go to a social event and need to drive a short time after. What precaution should you take?

Mark one answer

- [ ] A. Avoid drinking alcohol on an empty stomach
- [ ] B. Drink plenty of coffee after drinking alcohol
- [ ] C. Avoid drinking alcohol completely
- [ ] D. Drink plenty of milk before drinking alcohol

295 You take some cough medicine given to you by a friend. What should you do before driving?

Mark one answer

- [ ] A. Ask your friend if taking the medicine affected their driving
- [ ] B. Drink some strong coffee one hour before driving
- [ ] C. Check the label to see if the medicine will affect your driving
- [ ] D. Drive a short distance to see if the medicine is affecting your driving

296 You take the wrong route and find you are on a one-way street. You should

Mark one answer

- [ ] A. reverse out of the road
- [ ] B. turn round in a side road
- [ ] C. continue to the end of the road
- [ ] D. reverse into a driveway

297 Which THREE are likely to make you lose concentration while driving?

Mark three answers

- [ ] **A.** Looking at road maps
- [ ] **B.** Listening to loud music
- [ ] **C.** Using your windscreen washers
- [ ] **D.** Looking in your wing mirror
- [ ] **E.** Using a mobile phone

298 You are driving along this road. The driver on the left is reversing from a driveway. You should

Mark one answer

- [ ] **A.** move to the opposite side of the road
- [ ] **B.** drive through as you have priority
- [ ] **C.** sound your horn and be prepared to stop
- [ ] **D.** speed up and drive through quickly

299 You have been involved in an argument before starting your journey. This has made you feel angry. You should

Mark one answer

- [ ] **A.** start to drive, but open a window
- [ ] **B.** drive slower than normal and turn your radio on
- [ ] **C.** have an alcoholic drink to help you relax before driving
- [ ] **D.** calm down before you start to drive

300 You start to feel tired while driving. What should you do?

Mark one answer

- [ ] **A.** Increase your speed slightly
- [ ] **B.** Decrease your speed slightly
- [ ] **C.** Find a less busy route
- [ ] **D.** Pull over at a safe place to rest

301 You are driving on this dual carriageway. Why may you need to slow down?

Mark one answer

- [ ] **A.** There is a broken white line in the centre
- [ ] **B.** There are solid white lines either side
- [ ] **C.** There are road works ahead of you
- [ ] **D.** There are no footpaths

TIP It is tragic but true that people have been killed or seriously injured when struck by a vehicle being driven slowly in reverse gear. Young children, elderly and disabled people are especially vulnerable, often because they may not be aware of any danger. If in doubt get out and check!

302 You have just been overtaken by this motorcyclist who is cutting in sharply. You should

Mark one answer
- A. sound the horn
- B. brake firmly
- C. keep a safe gap
- D. flash your lights

303 You are about to drive home. You cannot find the glasses you need to wear. You should

Mark one answer
- A. drive home slowly, keeping to quiet roads
- B. borrow a friend's glasses and use those
- C. drive home at night, so that the lights will help you
- D. find a way of getting home without driving

304 Which THREE result from drinking alcohol?

Mark three answers
- A. Less control
- B. A false sense of confidence
- C. Faster reactions
- D. Poor judgement of speed
- E. Greater awareness of danger

305 Which THREE of these are likely effects of drinking alcohol?

Mark three answers
- A. Reduced co-ordination
- B. Increased confidence
- C. Poor judgement
- D. Increased concentration
- E. Faster reactions
- F. Colour blindness

306 How does alcohol affect you?

Mark one answer
- A. It speeds up your reactions
- B. It increases your awareness
- C. It improves your co-ordination
- D. It reduces your concentration

307 Your doctor has given you a course of medicine. Why should you ask how it will affect you?

Mark one answer
- A. Drugs make you a better driver by quickening your reactions
- B. You will have to let your insurance company know about the medicine
- C. Some types of medicine can cause your reactions to slow down
- D. The medicine you take may affect your hearing

308
You are not sure if your cough medicine will affect you. What TWO things could you do?

Mark two answers
- [ ] **A.** Ask your doctor
- [ ] **B.** Check the medicine label
- [ ] **C.** Drive if you feel alright
- [ ] **D.** Ask a friend or relative for advice

309
You are on a motorway. You feel tired. You should

Mark one answer
- [ ] **A.** carry on but go slowly
- [ ] **B.** leave the motorway at the next exit
- [ ] **C.** complete your journey as quickly as possible
- [ ] **D.** stop on the hard shoulder

310
You find that you need glasses to read vehicle number plates at the required distance. When MUST you wear them?

Mark one answer
- [ ] **A.** Only in bad weather conditions
- [ ] **B.** At all times when driving
- [ ] **C.** Only when you think it necessary
- [ ] **D.** Only in bad light or at night time

311
Which TWO things would help to keep you alert during a long journey?

Mark two answers
- [ ] **A.** Finishing your journey as fast as you can
- [ ] **B.** Keeping off the motorways and using country roads
- [ ] **C.** Making sure that you get plenty of fresh air
- [ ] **D.** Making regular stops for refreshments

312
Which of the following types of glasses should NOT be worn when driving at night?

Mark one answer
- [ ] **A.** Half-moon
- [ ] **B.** Round
- [ ] **C.** Bi-focal
- [ ] **D.** Tinted

313
Drinking any amount of alcohol is likely to

Mark three answers
- [ ] **A.** slow down your reactions to hazards
- [ ] **B.** increase the speed of your reactions
- [ ] **C.** worsen your judgement of speed
- [ ] **D.** improve your awareness of danger
- [ ] **E.** give a false sense of confidence

314
What else can seriously affect your concentration, other than alcoholic drinks?

Mark three answers
- [ ] **A.** Drugs
- [ ] **B.** Tiredness
- [ ] **C.** Tinted windows
- [ ] **D.** Contact lenses
- [ ] **E.** Loud music

315
As a driver you find that your eyesight has become very poor. Your optician says they cannot help you. The law says that you should tell

Mark one answer
- [ ] **A.** the licensing authority
- [ ] **B.** your own doctor
- [ ] **C.** the local police station
- [ ] **D.** another optician

316 For which of these may you use hazard warning lights?

Mark one answer

- [ ] A. When driving on a motorway to warn traffic behind of a hazard ahead
- [ ] B. When you are double-parked on a two-way road
- [ ] C. When your direction indicators are not working
- [ ] D. When warning oncoming traffic that you intend to stop

317 When should you use hazard warning lights?

Mark one answer

- [ ] A. When you are double-parked on a two-way road
- [ ] B. When your direction indicators are not working
- [ ] C. When warning oncoming traffic that you intend to stop
- [ ] D. When your vehicle has broken down and is causing an obstruction

TIP A blind person will usually carry a **white stick** to alert you to their presence. If the stick has a **red band**, this means that the person is also deaf, so will have no warning of an approaching car either visually or from engine noise.

318 You want to turn left at this junction. The view of the main road is restricted. What should you do?

Mark one answer

- [ ] A. Stay well back and wait to see if something comes
- [ ] B. Build up your speed so that you can emerge quickly
- [ ] C. Stop and apply the handbrake even if the road is clear
- [ ] D. Approach slowly and edge out until you can see more clearly

319 You are driving on a motorway. The traffic ahead is braking sharply because of an accident. How could you warn following traffic?

Mark one answer

- [ ] A. Briefly use the hazard warning lights
- [ ] B. Switch on the hazard warning lights continuously
- [ ] C. Briefly use the rear fog lights
- [ ] D. Switch on the headlamps continuously

320 When may you use hazard warning lights?

Mark one answer

- [ ] **A.** To park alongside another car
- [ ] **B.** To park on double yellow lines
- [ ] **C.** When you are being towed
- [ ] **D.** When you have broken down

321 Hazard warning lights should be used when vehicles are

Mark one answer

- [ ] **A.** broken down and causing an obstruction
- [ ] **B.** faulty and moving slowly
- [ ] **C.** being towed along a road
- [ ] **D.** reversing into a side road

322 When driving a car fitted with automatic transmission what would you use 'kick down' for?

Mark one answer

- [ ] **A.** Cruise control
- [ ] **B.** Quick acceleration
- [ ] **C.** Slow braking
- [ ] **D.** Fuel economy

TIP Research shows that male drivers (aged 18–30) are more at risk of falling asleep at the wheel than other drivers. They may keep late hours and be lacking in sleep; they tend to drive fast and be over-confident of their ability; and they are less likely to stop and take a break.

323 Which sign means that there may be people walking along the road?

Mark one answer

A.

B.

C.

D.

324 You are turning left at a junction. Pedestrians have started to cross the road. You should

Mark one answer

A. go on, giving them plenty of room

B. stop and wave at them to cross

C. blow your horn and proceed

D. give way to them

325 You are turning left from a main road into a side road. People are already crossing the road into which you are turning. You should

Mark one answer

A. continue, as it is your right of way

B. signal to them to continue crossing

C. wait and allow them to cross

D. sound your horn to warn them of your presence

326 You are at a road junction, turning into a minor road. There are pedestrians crossing the minor road. You should

Mark one answer

A. stop and wave the pedestrians across

B. sound your horn to let the pedestrians know that you are there

C. give way to the pedestrians who are already crossing

D. carry on; the pedestrians should give way to you

327
You are turning left into a side road. What hazards should you be especially aware of?

Mark one answer
- A. One-way street
- B. Pedestrians
- C. Traffic congestion
- D. Parked vehicles

328
You intend to turn right into a side road. Just before turning you should check for motorcyclists who might be

Mark one answer
- A. overtaking on your left
- B. following you closely
- C. emerging from the side road
- D. overtaking on your right

329
A toucan crossing is different from other crossings because

Mark one answer
- A. moped riders can use it
- B. it is controlled by a traffic warden
- C. it is controlled by two flashing lights
- D. cyclists can use it

330
At toucan crossings

Mark two answers
- A. there is no flashing amber light
- B. cyclists are not permitted
- C. there is a continuously flashing amber beacon
- D. pedestrians and cyclists may cross
- E. you only stop if someone is waiting to cross

331
What does this sign tell you?

Mark one answer
- A. No cycling
- B. Cycle route ahead
- C. Route for cycles only
- D. End of cycle route

332
How will a school crossing patrol signal you to stop?

Mark one answer
- A. By pointing to children on the opposite pavement
- B. By displaying a red light
- C. By displaying a stop sign
- D. By giving you an arm signal

333
Where would you see this sign?

Mark one answer
- A. In the window of a car taking children to school
- B. At the side of the road
- C. At playground areas
- D. On the rear of a school bus or coach

334 Which sign tells you that pedestrians may be walking in the road as there is no pavement?

Mark one answer

A.

B.

C.

D.

335 What does this sign mean?

Mark one answer

- A. No route for pedestrians and cyclists
- B. A route for pedestrians only
- C. A route for cyclists only
- D. A route for pedestrians and cyclists

336 You see a pedestrian with a white stick and red band. This means that the person is

Mark one answer

- A. physically disabled
- B. deaf only
- C. blind only
- D. deaf and blind

337 What action would you take when elderly people are crossing the road?

Mark one answer

- A. Wave them across so they know that you have seen them
- B. Be patient and allow them to cross in their own time
- C. Rev the engine to let them know that you are waiting
- D. Tap the horn in case they are hard of hearing

338 You see two elderly pedestrians about to cross the road ahead. You should

Mark one answer

- A. expect them to wait for you to pass
- B. speed up to get past them quickly
- C. stop and wave them across the road
- D. be careful, they may misjudge your speed

339 What does this sign mean?

Mark one answer

- A. Contraflow pedal cycle lane
- B. With-flow pedal cycle lane
- C. Pedal cycles and buses only
- D. No pedal cycles or buses

340 You are coming up to a roundabout. A cyclist is signalling to turn right. What should you do?

Mark one answer

- A. Overtake on the right
- B. Give a horn warning
- C. Signal the cyclist to move across
- D. Give the cyclist plenty of room

341 You are approaching this roundabout and see the cyclist signal right. Why is the cyclist keeping to the left?

Mark one answer

- A. It is a quicker route for the cyclist
- B. The cyclist is going to turn left instead
- C. The cyclist thinks *The Highway Code* does not apply to bicycles
- D. The cyclist is slower and more vulnerable

342 When you are overtaking a cyclist you should leave as much room as you would give to a car. What is the main reason for this?

Mark one answer

- A. The cyclist might change lanes
- B. The cyclist might get off the bike
- C. The cyclist might swerve
- D. The cyclist might have to make a right turn

343 Which TWO should you allow extra room when overtaking?

Mark two answers

- A. Motorcycles
- B. Tractors
- C. Bicycles
- D. Road-sweeping vehicles

344 Why should you look particularly for motorcyclists and cyclists at junctions?

Mark one answer

- A. They may want to turn into the side road
- B. They may slow down to let you turn
- C. They are harder to see
- D. They might not see you turn

345 You are waiting to come out of a side road. Why should you watch carefully for motorcycles?

Mark one answer

- A. Motorcycles are usually faster than cars
- B. Police patrols often use motorcycles
- C. Motorcycles are small and hard to see
- D. Motorcycles have right of way

346 In daylight, an approaching motorcyclist is using a dipped headlight. Why?

Mark one answer

- A. So that the rider can be seen more easily
- B. To stop the battery overcharging
- C. To improve the rider's vision
- D. The rider is inviting you to proceed

347 Motorcyclists should wear bright clothing mainly because

Mark one answer
- A. they must do so by law
- B. it helps keep them cool in summer
- C. the colours are popular
- D. drivers often do not see them

348 There is a slow-moving motorcyclist ahead of you. You are unsure what the rider is going to do. You should

Mark one answer
- A. pass on the left
- B. pass on the right
- C. stay behind
- D. move closer

349 Motorcyclists will often look round over their right shoulder just before turning right. This is because

Mark one answer
- A. they need to listen for following traffic
- B. motorcycles do not have mirrors
- C. looking around helps them balance as they turn
- D. they need to check for traffic in their blind area

350 At road junctions which of the following are most vulnerable?

Mark three answers
- A. Cyclists
- B. Motorcyclists
- C. Pedestrians
- D. Car drivers
- E. Lorry drivers

351 Motorcyclists are particularly vulnerable

Mark one answer
- A. when moving off
- B. on dual carriageways
- C. when approaching junctions
- D. on motorways

352 An injured motorcyclist is lying unconscious in the road. You should

Mark one answer
- A. remove the safety helmet
- B. seek medical assistance
- C. move the person off the road
- D. remove the leather jacket

353 You notice horse riders in front. What should you do FIRST?

Mark one answer
- A. Pull out to the middle of the road
- B. Be prepared to slow down
- C. Accelerate around them
- D. Signal right

354 You are approaching a roundabout. There are horses just ahead of you. You should

Mark two answers
- A. be prepared to stop
- B. treat them like any other vehicle
- C. give them plenty of room
- D. accelerate past as quickly as possible
- E. sound your horn as a warning

355 Which THREE should you do when passing sheep on a road?

Mark three answers
- A. Allow plenty of room
- B. Go very slowly
- C. Pass quickly but quietly
- D. Be ready to stop
- E. Briefly sound your horn

356 At night you see a pedestrian wearing reflective clothing and carrying a bright red light. What does this mean?

Mark one answer
- A. You are approaching road works
- B. You are approaching an organised walk
- C. You are approaching a slow-moving vehicle
- D. You are approaching an accident black spot

357 As you approach a pelican crossing the lights change to green. Elderly people are half-way across. You should

Mark one answer
- A. wave them to cross as quickly as they can
- B. rev your engine to make them hurry
- C. flash your lights in case they have not heard you
- D. wait because they will take longer to cross

358 There are flashing amber lights under a school warning sign. What action should you take?

Mark one answer
- A. Reduce speed until you are clear of the area
- B. Keep up your speed and sound the horn
- C. Increase your speed to clear the area quickly
- D. Wait at the lights until they change to green

359 Which of the following types of crossing can detect when people are on them?

Mark one answer
- A. Pelican
- B. Toucan
- C. Zebra
- D. Puffin

TIP It's the motorist's responsibility to look out for hazards and give pedestrians plenty of room.

360 You are approaching this crossing. You should

Mark one answer
- **A.** prepare to slow down and stop
- **B.** stop and wave the pedestrians across
- **C.** speed up and pass by quickly
- **D.** drive on unless the pedestrians step out

361 You see a pedestrian with a dog. The dog has a bright orange lead and collar. This especially warns you that the pedestrian is

Mark one answer
- **A.** elderly
- **B.** dog training
- **C.** colour blind
- **D.** deaf

362 These road markings must be kept clear to allow

W-SCHOOL KEEP CLEAR-W

Mark one answer
- **A.** schoolchildren to be dropped off
- **B.** for teachers to park
- **C.** schoolchildren to be picked up
- **D.** a clear view of the crossing area

363 You must not stop on these road markings because you may obstruct

W-SCHOOL KEEP CLEAR-W

Mark one answer
- **A.** children's view of the crossing area
- **B.** teachers' access to the school
- **C.** delivery vehicles' access to the school
- **D.** emergency vehicles' access to the school

364 The left-hand pavement is closed due to street repairs. What should you do?

Mark one answer
- **A.** Watch out for pedestrians walking in the road
- **B.** Use your right-hand mirror more often
- **C.** Speed up to get past the road works quicker
- **D.** Position close to the left-hand kerb

365 Where would you see this sign?

Mark one answer
- **A.** Near a school crossing
- **B.** At a playground entrance
- **C.** On a school bus
- **D.** At a 'pedestrians only' area

366 You are following a motorcyclist on an uneven road. You should

Mark one answer

- [ ] **A.** allow less room so you can be seen in their mirrors
- [ ] **B.** overtake immediately
- [ ] **C.** allow extra room in case they swerve to avoid pot-holes
- [ ] **D.** allow the same room as normal because road surfaces do not affect motorcyclists

367 You are following two cyclists. They approach a roundabout in the left-hand lane. In which direction should you expect the cyclists to go?

Mark one answer

- [ ] **A.** Left
- [ ] **B.** Right
- [ ] **C.** Any direction
- [ ] **D.** Straight ahead

368 You are travelling behind a moped. You want to turn left just ahead. You should

Mark one answer

- [ ] **A.** overtake the moped before the junction
- [ ] **B.** pull alongside the moped and stay level until just before the junction
- [ ] **C.** sound your horn as a warning and pull in front of the moped
- [ ] **D.** stay behind until the moped has passed the junction

369 Which THREE of the following are hazards motorcyclists present in queues of traffic?

Mark three answers

- [ ] **A.** Cutting in just in front of you
- [ ] **B.** Riding in single file
- [ ] **C.** Passing very close to you
- [ ] **D.** Riding with their headlight on dipped beam
- [ ] **E.** Filtering between the lanes

370 You see a horse rider as you approach a roundabout. They are signalling right but keeping well to the left. You should

Mark one answer

- [ ] **A.** proceed as normal
- [ ] **B.** keep close to them
- [ ] **C.** cut in front of them
- [ ] **D.** stay well back

371 How would you react to drivers who appear to be inexperienced?

Mark one answer

- [ ] **A.** Sound your horn to warn them of your presence
- [ ] **B.** Be patient and prepare for them to react more slowly
- [ ] **C.** Flash your headlights to indicate that it is safe for them to proceed
- [ ] **D.** Overtake them as soon as possible

372 You are following a learner driver who stalls at a junction. You should

Mark one answer

- A. be patient as you expect them to make mistakes
- B. stay very close behind and flash your headlights
- C. start to rev your engine if they take too long to restart
- D. immediately steer around them and drive on

373 You are on a country road. What should you expect to see coming towards you on YOUR side of the road?

Mark one answer

- A. Motorcycles
- B. Bicycles
- C. Pedestrians
- D. Horse riders

374 You are turning left into a side road. Pedestrians are crossing the road near the junction. You must

Mark one answer

- A. wave them on
- B. sound your horn
- C. switch on your hazard lights
- D. wait for them to cross

375 You are following a car driven by an elderly driver. You should

Mark one answer

- A. expect the driver to drive badly
- B. flash your lights and overtake
- C. be aware that the driver's reactions may not be as fast as yours
- D. stay very close behind but be careful

376 You are following a cyclist. You wish to turn left just ahead. You should

Mark one answer

- A. overtake the cyclist before the junction
- B. pull alongside the cyclist and stay level until after the junction
- C. hold back until the cyclist has passed the junction
- D. go around the cyclist on the junction

377 A horse rider is in the left-hand lane approaching a roundabout. You should expect the rider to

Mark one answer

- A. go in any direction
- B. turn right
- C. turn left
- D. go ahead

378 You have just passed your test. How can you decrease your risk of accidents on the motorway?

Mark one answer
- [ ] **A.** By keeping up with the car in front
- [ ] **B.** By never going over 40mph
- [ ] **C.** By staying only in the left-hand lane
- [ ] **D.** By taking further training

379 Powered vehicles used by disabled people are small and hard to see. How do they give early warning when on a dual carriageway?

Mark one answer
- [ ] **A.** They will have a flashing red light
- [ ] **B.** They will have a flashing green light
- [ ] **C.** They will have a flashing blue light
- [ ] **D.** They will have a flashing amber light

380 You should never attempt to overtake a cyclist

Mark one answer
- [ ] **A.** just before you turn left
- [ ] **B.** on a left-hand bend
- [ ] **C.** on a one-way street
- [ ] **D.** on a dual carriageway

381 Ahead of you there is a moving vehicle with a flashing amber beacon. This means it is

Mark one answer
- [ ] **A.** slow moving
- [ ] **B.** broken down
- [ ] **C.** a doctor's car
- [ ] **D.** a school crossing patrol

382 You want to reverse into a side road. You are not sure that the area behind your car is clear. What should you do?

Mark one answer
- [ ] **A.** Look through the rear window only
- [ ] **B.** Get out and check
- [ ] **C.** Check the mirrors only
- [ ] **D.** Carry on, assuming it is clear

383 You are about to reverse into a side road. A pedestrian wishes to cross behind you. You should

Mark one answer
- [ ] **A.** wave to the pedestrian to stop
- [ ] **B.** give way to the pedestrian
- [ ] **C.** wave to the pedestrian to cross
- [ ] **D.** reverse before the pedestrian starts to cross

384 Who is especially in danger of not being seen as you reverse your car?

Mark one answer
- [ ] **A.** Motorcyclists
- [ ] **B.** Car drivers
- [ ] **C.** Cyclists
- [ ] **D.** Children

385 You are reversing around a corner when you notice a pedestrian walking behind you. What should you do?

Mark one answer
- [ ] **A.** Slow down and wave the pedestrian across
- [ ] **B.** Continue reversing and steer round the pedestrian
- [ ] **C.** Stop and give way
- [ ] **D.** Continue reversing and sound your horn

386
You want to turn right from a junction but your view is restricted by parked vehicles. What should you do?

Mark one answer
- A. Move out quickly, but be prepared to stop
- B. Sound your horn and pull out if there is no reply
- C. Stop, then move slowly forward until you have a clear view
- D. Stop, get out and look along the main road to check

387
You are at the front of a queue of traffic waiting to turn right into a side road. Why is it important to check your right mirror just before turning?

Mark one answer
- A. To look for pedestrians about to cross
- B. To check for overtaking vehicles
- C. To make sure the side road is clear
- D. To check for emerging traffic

388
What must a driver do at a pelican crossing when the amber light is flashing?

Mark one answer
- A. Signal the pedestrian to cross
- B. Always wait for the green light before proceeding
- C. Give way to any pedestrians on the crossing
- D. Wait for the red-and-amber light before proceeding

389
You have stopped at a pelican crossing. A disabled person is crossing slowly in front of you. The lights have now changed to green. You should

Mark two answers
- A. allow the person to cross
- B. drive in front of the person
- C. drive behind the person
- D. sound your horn
- E. be patient
- F. edge forward slowly

390
You are driving past parked cars. You notice a wheel of a bicycle sticking out between them. What should you do?

Mark one answer
- A. Accelerate past quickly and sound your horn
- B. Slow down and wave the cyclist across
- C. Brake sharply and flash your headlights
- D. Slow down and be prepared to stop for a cyclist

TIP **Pass Plus** is a scheme set up in 1995 by the Driving Standards Agency and the Department of the Environment, Transport and the Regions. Planned in consultation with driving instructors and the insurance industry, it's aimed at encouraging people to go on training to *improve* their standard of driving during the first year after they pass their test.

391

You are driving past a line of parked cars. You notice a ball bouncing out into the road ahead. What should you do?

Mark one answer

- **A.** Continue driving at the same speed and sound your horn
- **B.** Continue driving at the same speed and flash your headlights
- **C.** Slow down and be prepared to stop for children
- **D.** Stop and wave the children across to fetch their ball

392

You want to turn right from a main road into a side road. Just before turning you should

Mark one answer

- **A.** cancel your right-turn signal
- **B.** select first gear
- **C.** check for traffic overtaking on your right
- **D.** stop and set the handbrake

393

You are driving in slow-moving queues of traffic. Just before changing lane you should

Mark one answer

- **A.** sound the horn
- **B.** look for motorcyclists filtering through the traffic
- **C.** give a 'slowing down' arm signal
- **D.** change down to first gear

394

You are driving in town. There is a bus at the bus stop on the other side of the road. Why should you be careful?

Mark one answer

- **A.** The bus may have broken down
- **B.** Pedestrians may come from behind the bus
- **C.** The bus may move off suddenly
- **D.** The bus may remain stationary

395

How should you overtake horse riders?

Mark one answer

- **A.** Drive up close and overtake as soon as possible
- **B.** Speed is not important but allow plenty of room
- **C.** Use your horn just once to warn them
- **D.** Drive slowly and leave plenty of room

396

A friend wants to teach you to drive a car. They MUST

Mark one answer

- **A.** be over 21 and have held a full licence for at least two years
- **B.** be over 18 and hold an advanced driver's certificate
- **C.** be over 18 and have fully comprehensive insurance
- **D.** be over 21 and have held a full licence for at least three years

397

You are dazzled at night by a vehicle behind you. You should

Mark one answer

- **A.** set your mirror to anti-dazzle
- **B.** set your mirror to dazzle the other driver
- **C.** brake sharply to a stop
- **D.** switch your rear lights on and off

398
You have a collision whilst your car is moving. What is the first thing you must do?

Mark one answer
- A. Stop only if there are injured people
- B. Call the emergency services
- C. Stop at the scene of the accident
- D. Call your insurance company

399
Yellow zigzag lines on the road outside schools mean

W-SCHOOL KEEP CLEAR-W

Mark one answer
- A. sound your horn to alert other road users
- B. stop to allow children to cross
- C. you must not wait or park on these lines
- D. you must not drive over these lines

400
What do these road markings outside a school mean?

W-SCHOOL KEEP CLEAR-W

Mark one answer
- A. You may park here if you are a teacher
- B. Sound your horn before parking
- C. When parking use your hazard warning lights
- D. You must not wait or park your vehicle here

401
You are driving on a main road. You intend to turn right into a side road. Just before turning you should

Mark one answer
- A. adjust your interior mirror
- B. flash your headlamps
- C. steer over to the left
- D. check for traffic overtaking on your right

402
Why should you allow extra room when overtaking a motorcyclist on a windy day?

Mark one answer
- A. The rider may turn off suddenly to get out of the wind
- B. The rider may be blown across in front of you
- C. The rider may stop suddenly
- D. The rider may be travelling faster than normal

403
Which age group of drivers is most likely to be involved in a road accident?

Mark one answer
- A. 36 to 45-year-olds
- B. 55-year-olds and over
- C. 46 to 55-year-olds
- D. 17 to 25-year-olds

TIP Remember: part of learning to drive safely is being able to control the car at very slow speeds, as when following a cyclist.

404
You are driving towards a zebra crossing. Waiting to cross is a person in a wheelchair. You should

Mark one answer
- A. continue on your way
- B. wave to the person to cross
- C. wave to the person to wait
- D. be prepared to stop

405
Where in particular should you look out for motorcyclists?

Mark one answer
- A. In a filling station
- B. At a road junction
- C. Near a service area
- D. When entering a car park

406
Where should you take particular care to look out for motorcyclists and cyclists?

Mark one answer
- A. On dual carriageways
- B. At junctions
- C. At zebra crossings
- D. On one-way streets

407
The road outside this school is marked with yellow zigzag lines. What do these lines mean?

Mark one answer
- A. You may park on the lines when dropping off schoolchildren
- B. You may park on the lines when picking schoolchildren up
- C. You must not wait or park your vehicle here at all
- D. You must stay with your vehicle if you park here

TIP By far the greatest number of accidents occurs within 18 metres (20 yards) of a junction. T-junctions and staggered junctions have proved to be more dangerous than roundabouts, or even crossroads.

408
The road is wet. Why might a motorcyclist steer round drain covers on a bend?

Mark one answer
- [ ] **A.** To avoid puncturing the tyres on the edge of the drain covers
- [ ] **B.** To prevent the motorcycle sliding on the metal drain covers
- [ ] **C.** To help judge the bend using the drain covers as marker points
- [ ] **D.** To avoid splashing pedestrians on the pavement

409
You are about to overtake a slow-moving motorcyclist. Which one of these signs would make you take special care?

Mark one answer
- [ ] **A.**
- [ ] **B.**
- [ ] **C.**
- [ ] **D.**

410
You are waiting to emerge left from a minor road. A large vehicle is approaching from the right. You have time to turn, but you should wait. Why?

Mark one answer
- [ ] **A.** The large vehicle can easily hide an overtaking vehicle
- [ ] **B.** The large vehicle can turn suddenly
- [ ] **C.** The large vehicle is difficult to steer in a straight line
- [ ] **D.** The large vehicle can easily hide vehicles from the left

411
You are following a long vehicle. It approaches a crossroads and signals left, but moves out to the right. You should

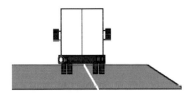

Mark one answer
- [ ] **A.** get closer in order to pass it quickly
- [ ] **B.** stay well back and give it room
- [ ] **C.** assume the signal is wrong and it is really turning right
- [ ] **D.** overtake as it starts to slow down

TIP If you cannot see the side mirrors of the long vehicle ahead, the driver is unaware you are there. Keep well back.

412

You are following a long vehicle approaching a crossroads. The driver signals right but moves close to the left-hand kerb. What should you do?

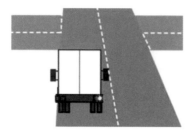

Mark one answer

- A. Warn the driver of the wrong signal
- B. Wait behind the long vehicle
- C. Report the driver to the police
- D. Overtake on the right-hand side

413

You are approaching a mini-roundabout. The long vehicle in front is signalling left but positioned over to the right. You should

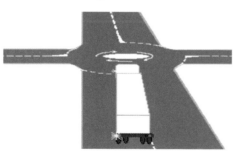

Mark one answer

- A. sound your horn
- B. overtake on the left
- C. follow the same course as the lorry
- D. keep well back

414

Before overtaking a large vehicle you should keep well back. Why is this?

Mark one answer

- A. To give acceleration space to overtake quickly on blind bends
- B. To get the best view of the road ahead
- C. To leave a gap in case the vehicle stops and rolls back
- D. To offer other drivers a safe gap if they want to overtake you

415

Why is passing a lorry more risky than passing a car?

Mark one answer

- A. Lorries are longer than cars
- B. Lorries may suddenly pull up
- C. The brakes of lorries are not as good
- D. Lorries climb hills more slowly

416

You are travelling behind a bus that pulls up at a bus stop. What should you do?

Mark two answers

- A. Accelerate past the bus sounding your horn
- B. Watch carefully for pedestrians
- C. Be ready to give way to the bus
- D. Pull in closely behind the bus

TIP Watch carefully for speed limits marked on the road – not just on traffic signs.

417 When you approach a bus signalling to move off from a bus stop you should

Mark one answer
- A. get past before it moves
- B. allow it to pull away, if it is safe to do so
- C. flash your headlights as you approach
- D. signal left and wave the bus on

418 Which of these vehicles is LEAST likely to be affected by crosswinds?

Mark one answer
- A. Cyclists
- B. Motorcyclists
- C. High-sided vehicles
- D. Cars

419 You are following a large lorry on a wet road. Spray makes it difficult to see. You should

Mark one answer
- A. drop back until you can see better
- B. put your headlights on full beam
- C. keep close to the lorry, away from the spray
- D. speed up and overtake quickly

420 Some two-way roads are divided into three lanes. Why are these particularly dangerous?

Mark one answer
- A. Traffic in both directions can use the middle lane to overtake
- B. Traffic can travel faster in poor weather conditions
- C. Traffic can overtake on the left
- D. Traffic uses the middle lane for emergencies only

421 What should you do as you approach this lorry?

Mark one answer
- A. Slow down and be prepared to wait
- B. Make the lorry wait for you
- C. Flash your lights at the lorry
- D. Move to the right-hand side of the road

TIP Box junctions were introduced to prevent blockages at crossroads and other junctions. The rule is: do not enter the box unless your exit is clear. Usually you will not stop in the yellow box unless, while your exit route is clear, you are caused to wait by oncoming traffic.

422

You are following a large articulated vehicle. It is going to turn left into a narrow road. What action should you take?

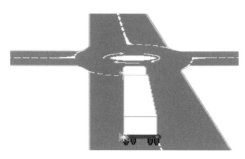

Mark one answer

- **A.** Move out and overtake on the right
- **B.** Pass on the left as the vehicle moves out
- **C.** Be prepared to stop behind
- **D.** Overtake quickly before the lorry moves out

423

You keep well back while waiting to overtake a large vehicle. A car fills the gap. You should

Mark one answer

- **A.** sound your horn
- **B.** drop back further
- **C.** flash your headlights
- **D.** start to overtake

424

At a junction you see this signal. It means

Mark one answer

- **A.** cars must stop
- **B.** trams must stop
- **C.** both trams and cars must stop
- **D.** both trams and cars can continue

425

You are following a large vehicle approaching crossroads. The driver signals to turn left. What should you do?

Mark one answer

- **A.** Overtake if you can leave plenty of room
- **B.** Overtake only if there are no oncoming vehicles
- **C.** Do not overtake until the vehicle begins to turn
- **D.** Do not overtake when at or approaching a junction

426

You are following a long lorry. The driver signals to turn left into a narrow road. What should you do?

Mark one answer

- **A.** Overtake on the left before the lorry reaches the junction
- **B.** Overtake on the right as soon as the lorry slows down
- **C.** Do not overtake unless you can see there is no oncoming traffic
- **D.** Do not overtake, stay well back and be prepared to stop

TIP Many drivers 'tailgate' in fog because the rear lights ahead give them a false sense of security. In fact, you should leave a much greater separation distance from the vehicle in front in any kind of adverse weather.

427 You wish to overtake a long, slow-moving vehicle on a busy road. You should

Mark one answer

- A. follow it closely and keep moving out to see the road ahead
- B. flash your headlights for the oncoming traffic to give way
- C. stay behind until the driver waves you past
- D. keep well back until you can see that it is clear

428 It is very windy. You are behind a motorcyclist who is overtaking a high-sided vehicle. What should you do?

Mark one answer

- A. Overtake the motorcyclist immediately
- B. Keep well back
- C. Stay level with the motorcyclist
- D. Keep close to the motorcyclist

429 It is very windy. You are about to overtake a motorcyclist. You should

Mark one answer

- A. overtake slowly
- B. allow extra room
- C. sound your horn
- D. keep close as you pass

430 You are towing a caravan. Which is the safest type of rear view mirror to use?

Mark one answer

- A. Interior wide-angle-view mirror
- B. Extended-arm side mirrors
- C. Ordinary door mirrors
- D. Ordinary interior mirror

431 You are driving downhill. There is a car parked on the other side of the road. Large, slow lorries are coming towards you. You should

Mark one answer

- A. keep going because you have the right of way
- B. slow down and give way
- C. speed up and get past quickly
- D. pull over on the right behind the parked car

432 You are driving in town. Ahead of you a bus is at a bus stop. Which TWO of the following should you do?

Mark two answers

- A. Be prepared to give way if the bus suddenly moves off
- B. Continue at the same speed but sound your horn as a warning
- C. Watch carefully for the sudden appearance of pedestrians
- D. Pass the bus as quickly as you possibly can

433 You are driving in heavy traffic on a wet road. Spray makes it difficult to be seen. You should use your

Mark two answers

- A. full beam headlights
- B. rear fog lights if visibility is less than 100 metres (328 feet)
- C. rear fog lights if visibility is more than 100 metres (328 feet)
- D. dipped headlights
- E. sidelights only

434 You are driving along this road. What should you be prepared to do?

Mark one answer

- A. Sound your horn and continue
- B. Slow down and give way
- C. Report the driver to the police
- D. Squeeze through the gap

435 You are on a wet motorway with surface spray. You should use

Mark one answer

- A. hazard flashers
- B. dipped headlights
- C. rear fog lights
- D. sidelights

436 As a driver why should you be more careful where trams operate?

Mark one answer

- A. Because they do not have a horn
- B. Because they do not stop for cars
- C. Because they do not have lights
- D. Because they cannot steer to avoid you

TIP If there's been a sudden downpour there may be water covering the road surface, making it difficult to control the car; and excessive speed may result in **aquaplaning**. It is rather like skidding, but on water, because the tyres cannot grip effectively. If you find yourself aquaplaning, take your foot off the accelerator and slow down gently. And keep a safe distance from the vehicle in front.

437

You are following a vehicle at a safe distance on a wet road. Another driver overtakes you and pulls into the gap you have left. What should you do?

Mark one answer
- A. Flash your headlights as a warning
- B. Try to overtake safely as soon as you can
- C. Drop back to regain a safe distance
- D. Stay close to the other vehicle until it moves on

438

In which THREE of these situations may you overtake another vehicle on the left?

Mark three answers
- A. When you are in a one-way street
- B. When approaching a motorway slip road where you will be turning off
- C. When the vehicle in front is signalling to turn right
- D. When a slower vehicle is travelling in the right hand lane of a dual carriageway
- E. In slow-moving traffic queues when traffic in the right-hand lane is moving more slowly

439

You are travelling in very heavy rain. Your overall stopping distance is likely to be

Mark one answer
- A. doubled
- B. halved
- C. up to ten times greater
- D. no different

440

Which TWO of the following are correct? When overtaking at night you should

Mark two answers
- A. wait until a bend so that you can see the oncoming headlights
- B. sound your horn twice before moving out
- C. be careful because you can see less
- D. beware of bends in the road ahead
- E. put headlights on full beam

441

When may you wait in a box junction?

Mark one answer
- A. When you are stationary in a queue of traffic
- B. When approaching a pelican crossing
- C. When approaching a zebra crossing
- D. When oncoming traffic prevents you turning right

442 Which of these plates normally appear with this road sign?

Mark one answer

A.
Humps for ½ mile

B.
Hump Bridge

C.
Low Bridge

D.
Soft Verge

443 Areas reserved for trams may have

Mark three answers

A. metal studs around them
B. white line markings
C. zigzag markings
D. a different coloured surface
E. yellow hatch markings
F. a different surface texture

444 Traffic calming measures are used to

Mark one answer

A. stop road rage
B. help overtaking
C. slow traffic down
D. help parking

445 Why should you always reduce your speed when travelling in fog?

Mark one answer

A. Because the brakes do not work as well
B. Because you could be dazzled by other people's fog lights
C. Because the engine is colder
D. Because it is more difficult to see events ahead

446 You are on a motorway in fog. The left-hand edge of the motorway can be identified by reflective studs. What colour are they?

Mark one answer

A. Green
B. Amber
C. Red
D. White

447 A rumble device is designed to

Mark two answers

A. give directions
B. prevent cattle escaping
C. alert you to low tyre pressure
D. alert you to a hazard
E. encourage you to reduce speed

448 You are on a narrow road at night. A slower-moving vehicle ahead has been signalling right for some time. What should you do?

Mark one answer

- A. Overtake on the left
- B. Flash your headlights before overtaking
- C. Signal right and sound your horn
- D. Wait for the signal to be cancelled before overtaking

449 Why should you test your brakes after this hazard?

Ford

Mark one answer

- A. Because you will be on a slippery road
- B. Because your brakes will be soaking wet
- C. Because you will have gone down a long hill
- D. Because you will have just crossed a long bridge

450 You have to make a journey in foggy conditions. You should

Mark one answer

- A. follow other vehicles' tail-lights closely
- B. avoid using dipped headlights
- C. leave plenty of time for your journey
- D. keep two seconds behind other vehicles

451 You are overtaking a car at night. You must be sure that

Mark one answer

- A. you flash your headlights before overtaking
- B. you select a higher gear
- C. you have switched your lights to full beam before overtaking
- D. you do not dazzle other road users

452 You see a vehicle coming towards you on a single track road. You should

Mark one answer

- A. go back to the main road
- B. do an emergency stop
- C. stop at a passing place
- D. put on your hazard warning lights

453 You are on a road which has speed humps. A driver in front is travelling slower than you. You should

Mark one answer

- A. sound your horn
- B. overtake as soon as you can
- C. flash your headlights
- D. slow down and stay behind

454 You are following other vehicles in fog with your lights on. How else can you reduce the chances of being involved in an accident?

Mark one answer

- [ ] **A.** Keep close to the vehicle in front
- [ ] **B.** Use your main beam instead of dipped headlights
- [ ] **C.** Keep together with the faster vehicles
- [ ] **D.** Reduce your speed and increase the gap

455 You see these markings on the road. Why are they there?

Mark one answer

- [ ] **A.** To show a safe distance between vehicles
- [ ] **B.** To keep the area clear of traffic
- [ ] **C.** To make you aware of your speed
- [ ] **D.** To warn you to change direction

456 When MUST you use dipped headlights during the day?

Mark one answer

- [ ] **A.** All the time
- [ ] **B.** Along narrow streets
- [ ] **C.** In poor visibility
- [ ] **D.** When parking

457 What are TWO main reasons why coasting downhill is wrong?

Mark two answers

- [ ] **A.** Fuel consumption will be higher
- [ ] **B.** The vehicle will pick up speed
- [ ] **C.** It puts more wear and tear on the tyres
- [ ] **D.** You have less braking and steering control
- [ ] **E.** It damages the engine

458 Hills can affect the performance of your vehicle. Which TWO apply when driving up steep hills?

Mark two answers

- [ ] **A.** Higher gears will pull better
- [ ] **B.** You will slow down sooner
- [ ] **C.** Overtaking will be easier
- [ ] **D.** The engine will work harder
- [ ] **E.** The steering will feel heavier

459 Why is coasting wrong?

Mark one answer

- [ ] **A.** It will cause the car to skid
- [ ] **B.** It will make the engine stall
- [ ] **C.** The engine will run faster
- [ ] **D.** There is no engine braking

460 You are driving on the motorway in windy conditions. When passing high-sided vehicles you should

Mark one answer

- [ ] **A.** increase your speed
- [ ] **B.** be wary of a sudden gust
- [ ] **C.** drive alongside very closely
- [ ] **D.** expect normal conditions

461 To correct a rear wheel skid you should

Mark one answer

- A. not steer at all
- B. steer away from it
- C. steer into it
- D. apply your handbrake

462 You have to make a journey in fog. What are the TWO most important things you should do before you set out?

Mark two answers

- A. Top up the radiator with antifreeze
- B. Make sure that you have a warning triangle in the vehicle
- C. Check that your lights are working
- D. Check the battery
- E. Make sure that the windows are clean

463 You are driving in fog. Why should you keep well back from the vehicle in front?

Mark one answer

- A. In case it changes direction suddenly
- B. In case its fog lights dazzle you
- C. In case it stops suddenly
- D. In case its brake lights dazzle you

464 You should switch your rear fog lights on when visibility drops below

Mark one answer

- A. your overall stopping distance
- B. ten car lengths
- C. 200 metres (656 feet)
- D. 100 metres (328 feet)

465 Whilst driving, the fog clears and you can see more clearly. You must remember to

Mark one answer

- A. switch off the fog lights
- B. reduce your speed
- C. switch off the demister
- D. close any open windows

466 You have to park on the road in fog. You should

Mark one answer

- A. leave sidelights on
- B. leave dipped headlights and fog lights on
- C. leave dipped headlights on
- D. leave main beam headlights on

467 On a foggy day you unavoidably have to park your car on the road. You should

Mark one answer

- A. leave your headlights on
- B. leave your fog lights on
- C. leave your sidelights on
- D. leave your hazard lights on

468 You are travelling at night. You are dazzled by headlights coming towards you. You should

Mark one answer

- A. pull down your sun visor
- B. slow down or stop
- C. switch on your main beam headlights
- D. put your hand over your eyes

469 Which of the following may apply when dealing with this hazard?

Mark four answers

- A. It could be more difficult in winter
- B. Use a low gear and drive slowly
- C. Use a high gear to prevent wheelspin
- D. Test your brakes afterwards
- E. Always switch on fog lamps
- F. There may be a depth gauge

470 Front fog lights may be used ONLY if

Mark one answer

- A. visibility is seriously reduced
- B. they are fitted above the bumper
- C. they are not as bright as the headlights
- D. an audible warning device is used

471 Front fog lights may be used ONLY if

Mark one answer

- A. your headlights are not working
- B. they are operated with rear fog lights
- C. they were fitted by the vehicle manufacturer
- D. visibility is seriously reduced

472 You are driving with your front fog lights switched on. Earlier fog has now cleared. What should you do?

Mark one answer

- A. Leave them on if other drivers have their lights on
- B. Switch them off as long as visibility remains good
- C. Flash them to warn oncoming traffic that it is foggy
- D. Drive with them on instead of your headlights

473 Front fog lights should be used ONLY when

Mark one answer

- A. travelling in very light rain
- B. visibility is seriously reduced
- C. daylight is fading
- D. driving after midnight

474 Why is it dangerous to leave rear fog lights on when they are not needed?

NI

Mark two answers

- A. Brake lights are less clear
- B. Following drivers can be dazzled
- C. Electrical systems could be overloaded
- D. Direction indicators may not work properly
- E. The battery could fail

475 You are driving on a clear dry night with your rear fog lights switched on. This may

Mark two answers NI

- A. reduce glare from the road surface
- B. make other drivers think you are braking
- C. give a better view of the road ahead
- D. dazzle following drivers
- E. help your indicators to be seen more clearly

476 You have just driven out of fog. Visibility is now good. You MUST

Mark one answer NI

- A. switch off all your fog lights
- B. keep your rear fog lights on
- C. keep your front fog lights on
- D. leave fog lights on in case fog returns

477 You forget to switch off your rear fog lights when the fog has cleared. This may

Mark three answers

- A. dazzle other road users
- B. reduce battery life
- C. cause brake lights to be less clear
- D. be breaking the law
- E. seriously affect engine power

478 You have been driving in thick fog which has now cleared. You must switch OFF your rear fog lights because

Mark one answer NI

- A. they use a lot of power from the battery
- B. they make your brake lights less clear
- C. they will cause dazzle in your rear-view mirrors
- D. they may not be properly adjusted

479 Front fog lights should be used

Mark one answer

- A. when visibility is reduced to 100 metres (328 feet)
- B. as a warning to oncoming traffic
- C. when driving during the hours of darkness
- D. in any conditions and at any time

480 Using rear fog lights in clear daylight will

Mark one answer

- A. be useful when towing a trailer
- B. give extra protection
- C. dazzle other drivers
- D. make following drivers keep back

481 Using front fog lights in clear daylight will

Mark one answer

- A. flatten the battery
- B. dazzle other drivers
- C. improve your visibility
- D. increase your awareness

482 You may use front fog lights with headlights ONLY when visibility is reduced to less than

Mark one answer

- A. 100 metres (328 feet)
- B. 200 metres (656 feet)
- C. 300 metres (984 feet)
- D. 400 metres (1,312 feet)

483 You may drive with front fog lights switched on

N 512 CTW

Mark one answer

- [ ] A. when visibility is less than 100 metres (328 feet)
- [ ] B. at any time to be noticed
- [ ] C. instead of headlights on high-speed roads
- [ ] D. when dazzled by the lights of oncoming vehicles

484 Chains can be fitted to your wheels to help prevent

Mark one answer

- [ ] A. damage to the road surface
- [ ] B. wear to the tyres
- [ ] C. skidding in deep snow
- [ ] D. the brakes locking

485 Pressing the clutch pedal down or rolling in neutral for too long while driving will

Mark one answer

- [ ] A. use more fuel
- [ ] B. cause the engine to overheat
- [ ] C. reduce your control
- [ ] D. improve tyre wear

486 How can you use the engine of your vehicle to control your speed?

Mark one answer

- [ ] A. By changing to a lower gear
- [ ] B. By selecting reverse gear
- [ ] C. By changing to a higher gear
- [ ] D. By selecting neutral

487 You are driving down a steep hill. Why could keeping the clutch down or selecting neutral for too long be dangerous?

Mark one answer

- [ ] A. Fuel consumption will be higher
- [ ] B. Your vehicle will pick up speed
- [ ] C. It will damage the engine
- [ ] D. It will wear tyres out more quickly

488 Why could keeping the clutch down or selecting neutral for long periods of time be dangerous?

Mark one answer

- [ ] A. Fuel spillage will occur
- [ ] B. Engine damage may be caused
- [ ] C. You will have less steering and braking control
- [ ] D. It will wear tyres out more quickly

489 You are driving on an icy road. What distance should you drive from the car in front?

Mark one answer

- **A.** four times the normal distance
- **B.** six times the normal distance
- **C.** eight times the normal distance
- **D.** ten times the normal distance

490 You are on a well-lit motorway at night. You must

Mark one answer

- **A.** use only your sidelights
- **B.** always use your headlights
- **C.** always use rear fog lights
- **D.** use headlights only in bad weather

491 You are on a motorway at night with other vehicles just ahead of you. Which lights should you have on?

Mark one answer

- **A.** Front fog lights
- **B.** Main beam headlights
- **C.** Sidelights only
- **D.** Dipped headlights

492 Which THREE of the following will affect your stopping distance?

Mark three answers

- **A.** How fast you are going
- **B.** The tyres on your vehicle
- **C.** The time of day
- **D.** The weather
- **E.** The street lighting

493 You are on a motorway at night. You MUST have your headlights switched on unless

Mark one answer **NI**

- **A.** there are vehicles close in front of you
- **B.** you are travelling below 50mph
- **C.** the motorway is lit
- **D.** your vehicle is broken down on the hard shoulder

494 You will feel the effects of engine braking when you

Mark one answer

- **A.** only use the handbrake
- **B.** only use neutral
- **C.** change to a lower gear
- **D.** change to a higher gear

495 Daytime visibility is poor but not seriously reduced. You should switch on

Mark one answer

- **A.** headlights and fog lights
- **B.** front fog lights
- **C.** dipped headlights
- **D.** rear fog lights

496 Why are vehicles fitted with rear fog lights?

Mark one answer

- **A.** To be seen when driving at high speed
- **B.** To use if broken down in a dangerous position
- **C.** To make them more visible in thick fog
- **D.** To warn drivers following closely to drop back

497 While you are driving in fog, it becomes necessary to use front fog lights. You should

Mark one answer

- **A.** only turn them on in heavy traffic conditions
- **B.** remember not to use them on motorways
- **C.** only use them on dual carriageways
- **D.** remember to switch them off as visibility improves

498 When snow is falling heavily you should

Mark one answer

- **A.** only drive with your hazard lights on
- **B.** not drive unless you have a mobile phone
- **C.** only drive when your journey is short
- **D.** not drive unless it is essential

499 You are driving down a long steep hill. You suddenly notice your brakes are not working as well as normal. What is the usual cause of this?

Mark one answer

- **A.** The brakes overheating
- **B.** Air in the brake fluid
- **C.** Oil on the brakes
- **D.** Badly adjusted brakes

TIP If you are being tailgated, gradually slow down to increase the gap between your vehicle and the one in front, allowing at least double the distance of the two-second rule. If you need to brake, allow for the following driver by braking early and gently, keeping an eye on the mirror. This is called **braking for two** – that is, for yourself and the tailgater.

500 Which FOUR of these must NOT use motorways?

Mark four answers

- A. Learner car drivers
- B. Motorcycles over 50cc
- C. Double-decker buses
- D. Farm tractors
- E. Horse riders
- F. Cyclists

501 Which FOUR of these must NOT use motorways?

Mark four answers

- A. Learner car drivers
- B. Motorcycles over 50cc
- C. Double-deck buses
- D. Farm tractors
- E. Learner motorcyclists
- F. Cyclists

502 Immediately after joining a motorway you should normally

Mark one answer

- A. try to overtake
- B. re-adjust your mirrors
- C. position your vehicle in the centre lane
- D. keep in the left lane

503 When joining a motorway you must always

Mark one answer

- A. use the hard shoulder
- B. stop at the end of the acceleration lane
- C. come to a stop before joining the motorway
- D. give way to traffic already on the motorway

504 What is the national speed limit for cars and motorcycles in the centre lane of a three-lane motorway?

Mark one answer

- A. 40mph
- B. 50mph
- C. 60mph
- D. 70mph

505 What is the national speed limit on motorways for cars and motorcycles?

Mark one answer

- A. 30mph
- B. 50mph
- C. 60mph
- D. 70mph

506 The left-hand lane on a three-lane motorway is for use by

Mark one answer

- A. any vehicle
- B. large vehicles only
- C. emergency vehicles only
- D. slow vehicles only

507 What is the right-hand lane used for on a three-lane motorway?

Mark one answer

- A. Emergency vehicles only
- B. Overtaking
- C. Vehicles towing trailers
- D. Coaches only

508 Which of these IS NOT allowed to travel in the right-hand lane of a three-lane motorway?

Mark one answer
- [ ] A. A small delivery van
- [ ] B. A motorcycle
- [ ] C. A vehicle towing a trailer
- [ ] D. A motorcycle and sidecar

509 You are travelling on a motorway. You decide you need a rest. You should

Mark two answers
- [ ] A. stop on the hard shoulder
- [ ] B. go to a service area
- [ ] C. park on the slip road
- [ ] D. park on the central reservation
- [ ] E. leave at the next exit

510 You break down on a motorway. You need to call for help. Why may it be better to use an emergency roadside telephone rather than a mobile phone?

Mark one answer   NI
- [ ] A. It connects you to a local garage
- [ ] B. Using a mobile phone will distract other drivers
- [ ] C. It allows easy location by the emergency services
- [ ] D. Mobile phones do not work on motorways

511 What should you use the hard shoulder of a motorway for?

Mark one answer
- [ ] A. Stopping in an emergency
- [ ] B. Leaving the motorway
- [ ] C. Stopping when you are tired
- [ ] D. Joining the motorway

512 After a breakdown you need to rejoin the main carriageway of a motorway from the hard shoulder. You should

Mark one answer
- [ ] A. move out on to the carriageway then build up your speed
- [ ] B. move out on to the carriageway using your hazard lights
- [ ] C. gain speed on the hard shoulder before moving out on to the carriageway
- [ ] D. wait on the hard shoulder until someone flashes their headlights at you

513 A crawler lane on a motorway is found

Mark one answer
- [ ] A. on a steep gradient
- [ ] B. before a service area
- [ ] C. before a junction
- [ ] D. along the hard shoulder

514 You are driving on a motorway. There are red flashing lights above every lane. You must

Mark one answer

- A. pull on to the hard shoulder
- B. slow down and watch for further signals
- C. leave at the next exit
- D. stop and wait

515 You are driving in the right-hand lane on a motorway. You see these overhead signs. This means

Mark one answer

- A. move to the left and reduce your speed to 50mph
- B. there are road works 50 metres (55 yards) ahead
- C. use the hard shoulder until you have passed the hazard
- D. leave the motorway at the next exit

516 What do these motorway signs show?

Mark one answer

- A. They are countdown markers to a bridge
- B. They are distance markers to the next telephone
- C. They are countdown markers to the next exit
- D. They warn of a police control ahead

517 On a motorway the amber reflective studs can be found between

Mark one answer

- A. the hard shoulder and the carriageway
- B. the acceleration lane and the carriageway
- C. the central reservation and the carriageway
- D. each pair of the lanes

518 What colour are the reflective studs between the lanes on a motorway?

Mark one answer

- A. Green
- B. Amber
- C. White
- D. Red

519 What colour are the reflective studs between a motorway and its slip road?

Mark one answer

- A. Amber
- B. White
- C. Green
- D. Red

520 You are allowed to stop on a motorway when you

Mark one answer

- A. need to walk and get fresh air
- B. wish to pick up hitch-hikers
- C. are told to do so by flashing red lights
- D. need to use a mobile telephone

521 You have broken down on a motorway. To find the nearest emergency telephone you should always walk

Mark one answer

- [ ] **A.** with the traffic flow
- [ ] **B.** facing oncoming traffic
- [ ] **C.** in the direction shown on the marker posts
- [ ] **D.** in the direction of the nearest exit

522 You are travelling along the left lane of a three-lane motorway. Traffic is joining from a slip road. You should

Mark one answer

- [ ] **A.** race the other vehicles
- [ ] **B.** move to another lane
- [ ] **C.** maintain a steady speed
- [ ] **D.** switch on your hazard flashers

523 You are joining a motorway. Why is it important to make full use of the slip road?

Mark one answer

- [ ] **A.** Because there is space available to turn round if you need to
- [ ] **B.** To allow you direct access to the overtaking lanes
- [ ] **C.** To build up a speed similar to traffic on the motorway
- [ ] **D.** Because you can continue on the hard shoulder

TIP Never underestimate how dangerous the hard shoulder can be. As many as one in eight road deaths happen there.

524 How should you use the emergency telephone on a motorway?

Mark one answer

- [ ] **A.** Stay close to the carriageway
- [ ] **B.** Face the oncoming traffic
- [ ] **C.** Keep your back to the traffic
- [ ] **D.** Stand on the hard shoulder

525 You are on a motorway. What colour are the reflective studs on the left of the carriageway?

Mark one answer

- [ ] **A.** Green
- [ ] **B.** Red
- [ ] **C.** White
- [ ] **D.** Amber

526 On a three-lane motorway which lane should you normally use?

Mark one answer

- [ ] **A.** Left
- [ ] **B.** Right
- [ ] **C.** Centre
- [ ] **D.** Either the right or centre

527 A basic rule when on motorways is

Mark one answer

- [ ] **A.** use the lane that has least traffic
- [ ] **B.** keep to the left lane unless overtaking
- [ ] **C.** overtake on the side that is clearest
- [ ] **D.** try to keep above 50mph to prevent congestion

528 When going through a contraflow system on a motorway you should

Mark one answer

- A. ensure that you do not exceed 30mph
- B. keep a good distance from the vehicle ahead
- C. switch lanes to keep the traffic flowing
- D. stay close to the vehicle ahead to reduce queues

529 You are on a three-lane motorway. There are red reflective studs on your left and white ones to your right. Where are you?

Mark one answer

- A. In the right-hand lane
- B. In the middle lane
- C. On the hard shoulder
- D. In the left-hand lane

530 When may you stop on a motorway?

Mark three answers

- A. If you have to read a map
- B. When you are tired and need a rest
- C. If red lights show above every lane
- D. When told to by the police
- E. If your mobile phone rings
- F. In an emergency or a breakdown

531 You are approaching road works on a motorway. What should you do?

Mark one answer

- A. Speed up to clear the area quickly
- B. Always use the hard shoulder
- C. Obey all speed limits
- D. Stay very close to the vehicle in front

532 On motorways you should never overtake on the left UNLESS

Mark one answer

- A. you can see well ahead that the hard shoulder is clear
- B. the traffic in the right-hand lane is signalling right
- C. you warn drivers behind by signalling left
- D. there is a queue of slow-moving traffic to your right that is moving slower than you are

533 You are towing a trailer on a motorway. What is your maximum speed limit?

Mark one answer

- A. 40mph
- B. 50mph
- C. 60mph
- D. 70mph

534 The left-hand lane of a motorway should be used for

Mark one answer
- A. breakdowns and emergencies only
- B. overtaking slower traffic in the other lanes
- C. slow vehicles only
- D. normal driving

535 You are driving on a motorway. You have to slow down quickly due to a hazard. You should

Mark one answer
- A. switch on your hazard lights
- B. switch on your headlights
- C. sound your horn
- D. flash your headlights

536 You get a puncture on the motorway. You manage to get your vehicle on to the hard shoulder. You should

Mark one answer
- A. change the wheel yourself immediately
- B. use the emergency telephone and call for assistance
- C. try to wave down another vehicle for help
- D. only change the wheel if you have a passenger to help you

537 You are driving on a motorway. By mistake, you go past the exit that you wanted to take. You should

Mark one answer
- A. carefully reverse on the hard shoulder
- B. carry on to the next exit
- C. carefully reverse in the left-hand lane
- D. make a U-turn at the next gap in the central reservation

538 Your vehicle breaks down on the hard shoulder of a motorway. You decide to use your mobile phone to call for help. You should

Mark one answer **NI**
- A. stand at the rear of the vehicle while making the call
- B. try to repair the vehicle yourself
- C. get out of the vehicle by the right-hand door
- D. check your location from the marker posts on the left

539 You are driving a car on a motorway. Unless signs show otherwise you must NOT exceed

Mark one answer
- A. 50mph
- B. 60mph
- C. 70mph
- D. 80mph

540 You are on a three-lane motorway towing a trailer. You may use the right-hand lane when

Mark one answer **NI**

- A. there are lane closures
- B. there is slow-moving traffic
- C. you can maintain a high speed
- D. large vehicles are in the left and centre lanes

541 You are on a motorway. There is a contraflow system ahead. What would you expect to find?

Mark one answer

- A. Temporary traffic lights
- B. Lower speed limits
- C. Wider lanes than normal
- D. Speed humps

542 You are driving at 70mph on a three-lane motorway. There is no traffic ahead. Which lane should you use?

Mark one answer

- A. Any lane
- B. Middle lane
- C. Right lane
- D. Left lane

543 Your vehicle has broken down on a motorway. You are not able to stop on the hard shoulder. What should you do?

Mark one answer

- A. Switch on your hazard warning lights
- B. Stop following traffic and ask for help
- C. Attempt to repair your vehicle quickly
- D. Stand behind your vehicle to warn others

544 Why is it particularly important to carry out a check on your vehicle before making a long motorway journey?

Mark one answer

- A. You will have to do more harsh braking on motorways
- B. Motorway service stations do not deal with breakdowns
- C. The road surface will wear down the tyres faster
- D. Continuous high speeds may increase the risk of your vehicle breaking down

545 For what reason may you use the right-hand lane of a motorway?

Mark one answer

- A. For keeping out of the way of lorries
- B. For driving at more than 70mph
- C. For turning right
- D. For overtaking other vehicles

546 On a motorway you may ONLY stop on the hard shoulder

Mark one answer

- [ ] **A.** in an emergency
- [ ] **B.** if you feel tired and need to rest
- [ ] **C.** if you accidentally go past the exit that you wanted to take
- [ ] **D.** to pick up a hitch-hiker

547 You are driving on a motorway. The car ahead shows its hazard lights for a short time. This tells you that

Mark one answer

- [ ] **A.** the driver wants you to overtake
- [ ] **B.** the other car is going to change lanes
- [ ] **C.** traffic ahead is slowing or stopping suddenly
- [ ] **D.** there is a police speed check ahead

548 The emergency telephones on a motorway are connected to the

Mark one answer

- [ ] **A.** ambulance service
- [ ] **B.** police control
- [ ] **C.** fire brigade
- [ ] **D.** breakdown service

549 You are intending to leave the motorway at the next exit. Before you reach the exit you should normally position your vehicle

Mark one answer

- [ ] **A.** in the middle lane
- [ ] **B.** in the left-hand lane
- [ ] **C.** on the hard shoulder
- [ ] **D.** in any lane

550 As a provisional licence holder you should not drive a car

Mark one answer

- [ ] **A.** over 30mph
- [ ] **B.** at night
- [ ] **C.** on the motorway
- [ ] **D.** with passengers in rear seats

TIP The first motorway sign-board, a mile before the exit, will only provide the road numbers and sometimes major town names. The half-mile sign gives major town names. Make sure you know in advance which junction number you're looking for.

551 What is the meaning of this sign?

Mark one answer
- A. Local speed limit applies
- B. No waiting on the carriageway
- C. National speed limit applies
- D. No entry to vehicular traffic

552 What is the national speed limit on a single carriageway road for cars and motorcycles?

Mark one answer
- A. 70mph
- B. 60mph
- C. 50mph
- D. 30mph

553 What is the national speed limit for cars and motorcycles on a dual carriageway?

Mark one answer
- A. 30mph
- B. 50mph
- C. 60mph
- D. 70mph

554 There are no speed limit signs on the road. How is a 30mph limit indicated?

Mark one answer
- A. By hazard warning lines
- B. By street lighting
- C. By pedestrian islands
- D. By double or single yellow lines

555 Where you see street lights but no speed limit signs the limit is usually

Mark one answer
- A. 30mph
- B. 40mph
- C. 50mph
- D. 60mph

556 What does this sign mean?

Mark one answer
- A. Minimum speed 30mph
- B. End of maximum speed
- C. End of minimum speed
- D. Maximum speed 30mph

557 There is a tractor ahead of you. You wish to overtake but you are NOT sure if it is safe to do so. You should

Mark one answer
- A. follow another overtaking vehicle through
- B. sound your horn to the slow vehicle to pull over
- C. speed through but flash your lights to oncoming traffic
- D. not overtake if you are in doubt

TIP When judging the probable actions of another vehicle at a junction, check for clues such as the position on the road of the other vehicle and the angle of the wheels.

558 Which three of the following are most likely to take an unusual course at roundabouts?

Mark three answers

- [ ] **A.** Horse riders
- [ ] **B.** Milk floats
- [ ] **C.** Delivery vans
- [ ] **D.** Long vehicles
- [ ] **E.** Estate cars
- [ ] **F.** Cyclists

559 In which FOUR places must you NOT park or wait?

Mark four answers

- [ ] **A.** On a dual carriageway
- [ ] **B.** At a bus stop
- [ ] **C.** On the slope of a hill
- [ ] **D.** Opposite a traffic island
- [ ] **E.** In front of someone else's drive
- [ ] **F.** On the brow of a hill

560 In which TWO places must you NOT park?

Mark two answers

- [ ] **A.** Near a school entrance
- [ ] **B.** Near a police station
- [ ] **C.** In a side road
- [ ] **D.** At a bus stop
- [ ] **E.** In a one-way street

561 On a clearway you must not stop

Mark one answer

- [ ] **A.** at any time
- [ ] **B.** when it is busy
- [ ] **C.** in the rush hour
- [ ] **D.** during daylight hours

562 What is the meaning of this sign?

Mark one answer

- [ ] **A.** No entry
- [ ] **B.** Waiting restrictions
- [ ] **C.** National speed limit
- [ ] **D.** School crossing patrol

563 You can park on the right-hand side of a road at night

Mark one answer

- [ ] **A.** in a one-way street
- [ ] **B.** with your sidelights on
- [ ] **C.** more than 10 metres (32 feet) from a junction
- [ ] **D.** under a lamppost

564 On a three-lane dual carriageway the right-hand lane can be used for

Mark one answer

- [ ] **A.** overtaking only, never turning right
- [ ] **B.** overtaking or turning right
- [ ] **C.** fast-moving traffic only
- [ ] **D.** turning right only, never overtaking

565 You are approaching a busy junction. There are several lanes with road markings. At the last moment you realise that you are in the wrong lane. You should

Mark one answer
- A. continue in that lane
- B. force your way across
- C. stop until the area has cleared
- D. use clear arm signals to cut across

566 Where may you overtake on a one-way street?

Mark one answer
- A. Only on the left-hand side
- B. Overtaking is not allowed
- C. Only on the right-hand side
- D. Either on the right or the left

567 When going straight ahead at a roundabout you should

Mark one answer
- A. indicate left before leaving the roundabout
- B. not indicate at any time
- C. indicate right when approaching the roundabout
- D. indicate left when approaching the roundabout

568 Which vehicle might have to use a different course to normal at roundabouts?

Mark one answer
- A. Sports car
- B. Van
- C. Estate car
- D. Long vehicle

569 You are going straight ahead at a roundabout. How should you signal?

Mark one answer
- A. Signal right on the approach and then left to leave the roundabout
- B. Signal left as you leave the roundabout
- C. Signal left on the approach to the roundabout and keep the signal on until you leave
- D. Signal left just after you pass the exit before the one you will take

570 You may only enter a box junction when

Mark one answer
- A. there are less than two vehicles in front of you
- B. the traffic lights show green
- C. your exit road is clear
- D. you need to turn left

TIP In your driving test, where there are lanes the examiner will check your position on the road; it's important not to be straddling two lanes at a time.

571 You may wait in a yellow box junction when

Mark one answer

- A. oncoming traffic is preventing you from turning right
- B. you are in a queue of traffic turning left
- C. you are in a queue of traffic to go ahead
- D. you are on a roundabout

572 You MUST stop when signalled to do so by which THREE of these?

Mark three answers

- A. A police officer
- B. A pedestrian
- C. A school crossing patrol
- D. A bus driver
- E. A red traffic light

TIP Did you know that you are allowed to have your seat belt unfastened when you are reversing? It's the only time you can do so when driving.

573 You will see these markers when approaching

Mark one answer

- A. the end of a motorway
- B. a concealed level crossing
- C. a concealed speed limit sign
- D. the end of a dual carriageway

574 Someone is waiting to cross at a zebra crossing. They are standing on the pavement. You should normally

Mark one answer

- A. go on quickly before they step on to the crossing
- B. stop before you reach the zigzag lines and let them cross
- C. stop, let them cross, wait patiently
- D. ignore them as they are still on the pavement

575 At toucan crossings, apart from pedestrians you should be aware of

Mark one answer

- A. emergency vehicles emerging
- B. buses pulling out
- C. trams crossing in front
- D. cyclists riding across

576 Who can use a toucan crossing?

Mark two answers

- A. Trains
- B. Cyclists
- C. Buses
- D. Pedestrians
- E. Trams

577 At a pelican crossing, what does a flashing amber light mean?

Mark one answer

- A. You must not move off until the lights stop flashing
- B. You must give way to pedestrians still on the crossing
- C. You can move off, even if pedestrians are still on the crossing
- D. You must stop because the lights are about to change to red

578 You are waiting at a pelican crossing. The red light changes to flashing amber. This means you must

Mark one answer

- A. wait for pedestrians on the crossing to clear
- B. move off immediately without any hesitation
- C. wait for the green light before moving off
- D. get ready and go when the continuous amber light shows

579 You are travelling on a well-lit road at night in a built-up area. By using dipped headlights you will be able to

Mark one answer

- A. see further along the road
- B. go at a much faster speed
- C. switch to main beam quickly
- D. be easily seen by others

580 When can you park on the left opposite these road markings?

Mark one answer

- A. If the line nearest to you is broken
- B. When there are no yellow lines
- C. To pick up or set down passengers
- D. During daylight hours only

581 You are intending to turn right at a crossroads. An oncoming driver is also turning right. It will normally be safer to

Mark one answer

- A. keep the other vehicle to your RIGHT and turn behind it (offside to offside)
- B. keep the other vehicle to your LEFT and turn in front of it (nearside to nearside)
- C. carry on and turn at the next junction instead
- D. hold back and wait for the other driver to turn first

582 You are on a road that has no traffic signs. There are street lights. What is the speed limit?

Mark one answer

- A. 20mph
- B. 30mph
- C. 40mph
- D. 60mph

583
You are going along a street with parked vehicles on the left-hand side. For which THREE reasons should you keep your speed down?

Mark three answers

- [ ] **A.** So that oncoming traffic can see you more clearly
- [ ] **B.** You may set off car alarms
- [ ] **C.** Vehicles may be pulling out
- [ ] **D.** Drivers' doors may open
- [ ] **E.** Children may run out from between the vehicles

584
You meet an obstruction on your side of the road. You should

Mark one answer

- [ ] **A.** carry on, you have priority
- [ ] **B.** give way to oncoming traffic
- [ ] **C.** wave oncoming vehicles through
- [ ] **D.** accelerate to get past first

585
You are on a two-lane dual carriageway. For which TWO of the following would you use the right-hand lane?

Mark two answers

- [ ] **A.** Turning right
- [ ] **B.** Normal progress
- [ ] **C.** Staying at the minimum allowed speed
- [ ] **D.** Constant high speed
- [ ] **E.** Overtaking slower traffic
- [ ] **F.** Mending punctures

586
Who has priority at an unmarked crossroads?

Mark one answer

- [ ] **A.** The larger vehicle
- [ ] **B.** No one has priority
- [ ] **C.** The faster vehicle
- [ ] **D.** The smaller vehicle

587
What is the nearest you may park to a junction?

Mark one answer **NI**

- [ ] **A.** 10 metres (32 feet)
- [ ] **B.** 12 metres (39 feet)
- [ ] **C.** 15 metres (49 feet)
- [ ] **D.** 20 metres (66 feet)

588
In which THREE places must you NOT park?

Mark three answers **NI**

- [ ] **A.** Near the brow of a hill
- [ ] **B.** At or near a bus stop
- [ ] **C.** Where there is no pavement
- [ ] **D.** Within 10 metres (32 feet) of a junction
- [ ] **E.** On a 40mph road

589
You are waiting at a level crossing. A train has passed but the lights keep flashing. You must

Mark one answer

- [ ] **A.** carry on waiting
- [ ] **B.** phone the signal operator
- [ ] **C.** edge over the stop line and look for trains
- [ ] **D.** park and investigate

590 You park overnight on a road with a 40mph speed limit. You should park

Mark one answer

- A. facing the traffic
- B. with parking lights on
- C. with dipped headlights on
- D. near a street light

591 The dual carriageway you are turning right on to has a very narrow central reserve. What should you do?

Mark one answer

- A. Proceed to the central reserve and wait
- B. Wait until the road is clear in both directions
- C. Stop in the first lane so that other vehicles give way
- D. Emerge slightly to show your intentions

592 At a crossroads there are no signs or road markings. Two vehicles approach. Which has priority?

Mark one answer

- A. Neither of the vehicles
- B. The vehicle travelling the fastest
- C. Oncoming vehicles turning right
- D. Vehicles approaching from the right

593 What does this sign tell you?

Mark one answer

- A. That it is a no-through road
- B. End of traffic calming zone
- C. Free parking zone ends
- D. No waiting zone ends

594 You are entering an area of road works. There is a temporary speed limit displayed. You should

Mark one answer

- A. not exceed the speed limit
- B. obey the limit only during rush hour
- C. ignore the displayed limit
- D. obey the limit except at night

595 You may drive over a footpath

Mark one answer

- A. to overtake slow-moving traffic
- B. when the pavement is very wide
- C. if no pedestrians are near
- D. to get into a property

596

A single-carriageway road has this sign. What is the maximum permitted speed for a car towing a trailer?

Mark one answer

- [ ] **A.** 30mph
- [ ] **C.** 50mph
- [ ] **B.** 40mph
- [ ] **D.** 60mph

597

You are towing a small caravan on a dual carriageway. You must not exceed

Mark one answer

- [ ] **A.** 50mph
- [ ] **C.** 70mph
- [ ] **B.** 40mph
- [ ] **D.** 60mph

598

You want to park and you see this sign. On the days and times shown you should

Mark one answer

- [ ] **A.** park in a bay and not pay
- [ ] **B.** park on yellow lines and pay
- [ ] **C.** park on yellow lines and not pay
- [ ] **D.** park in a bay and pay

Meter
ZONE

Mon - Fri
8.30 am - 6.30 pm
Saturday
8.30 am - 1.30 pm

599

As a car driver which THREE lanes are you NOT normally allowed to use?

Mark three answers

- [ ] **A.** Crawler lane
- [ ] **B.** Bus lane
- [ ] **C.** Overtaking lane
- [ ] **D.** Acceleration lane
- [ ] **E.** Cycle lane
- [ ] **F.** Tram lane

600

You are driving along a road that has a cycle lane. The lane is marked by a solid white line. This means that during its period of operation

Mark one answer

- [ ] **A.** the lane may be used for parking your car
- [ ] **B.** you may drive in that lane at any time
- [ ] **C.** the lane may be used when necessary
- [ ] **D.** you must not drive in that lane

601

A cycle lane is marked by a solid white line. You must not drive or park in it

Mark one answer

- [ ] **A.** at any time
- [ ] **B.** during the rush hour
- [ ] **C.** if a cyclist is using it
- [ ] **D.** during its period of operation

602

While driving, you intend to turn left into a minor road. On the approach you should

Mark one answer

- [ ] **A.** keep just left of the middle of the road
- [ ] **B.** keep in the middle of the road
- [ ] **C.** swing out wide just before turning
- [ ] **D.** keep well to the left of the road

603 You are waiting at a level crossing. The red warning lights continue to flash after a train has passed by. What should you do?

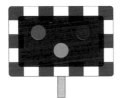

Mark one answer

- [ ] **A.** Get out and investigate
- [ ] **B.** Telephone the signal operator
- [ ] **C.** Continue to wait
- [ ] **D.** Drive across carefully

604 You are driving over a level crossing. The warning lights come on and a bell rings. What should you do?

Mark one answer

- [ ] **A.** Get everyone out of the vehicle immediately
- [ ] **B.** Stop and reverse back to clear the crossing
- [ ] **C.** Keep going and clear the crossing
- [ ] **D.** Stop immediately and use your hazard warning lights

605 You are on a busy main road and find that you are travelling in the wrong direction. What should you do?

Mark one answer

- [ ] **A.** Turn into a side road on the right and reverse into the main road
- [ ] **B.** Make a U-turn in the main road
- [ ] **C.** Make a 'three-point' turn in the main road
- [ ] **D.** Turn round in a side road

606 You may remove your seat belt when carrying out a manoeuvre that involves

Mark one answer

- [ ] **A.** reversing
- [ ] **B.** a hill start
- [ ] **C.** an emergency stop
- [ ] **D.** driving slowly

607 You must not reverse

Mark one answer

- [ ] **A.** for longer than necessary
- [ ] **B.** for more than a car's length
- [ ] **C.** into a side road
- [ ] **D.** in a built-up area

608 You are parked in a busy high street. What is the safest way to turn your vehicle around to go the opposite way?

Mark one answer

- [ ] **A.** Find a quiet side road to turn round in
- [ ] **B.** Drive into a side road and reverse into the main road
- [ ] **C.** Get someone to stop the traffic
- [ ] **D.** Do a U-turn

609 When you are NOT sure that it is safe to reverse your vehicle you should

Mark one answer

- A. use your horn
- B. rev your engine
- C. get out and check
- D. reverse slowly

610 When may you reverse from a side road into a main road?

Mark one answer

- A. Only if both roads are clear of traffic
- B. Not at any time
- C. At any time
- D. Only if the main road is clear of traffic

611 You want to turn right at a box junction. There is oncoming traffic. You should

Mark one answer

- A. wait in the box junction if your exit is clear
- B. wait before the junction until it is clear of all traffic
- C. drive on, you cannot turn right at a box junction
- D. drive slowly into the box junction when signalled by oncoming traffic

612 You are reversing your vehicle into a side road. When would the greatest hazard to passing traffic occur?

Mark one answer

- A. After you've completed the manoeuvre
- B. Just before you actually begin to manoeuvre
- C. After you've entered the side road
- D. When the front of your vehicle swings out

613 You are driving on a road that has a cycle lane. The lane is marked by a broken white line. This means that

Mark two answers

- A. you should not drive in the lane unless it is unavoidable
- B. you should not park in the lane unless it is unavoidable
- C. you can drive in the lane at any time
- D. the lane must be used by motorcyclists in heavy traffic

614 Where is the safest place to park your vehicle at night?

Mark one answer

- A. In a garage
- B. On a busy road
- C. In a quiet car park
- D. Near a red route

615 To help keep your vehicle secure at night where should you park?

Mark one answer

- A. Near a police station
- B. In a quiet road
- C. On a red route
- D. In a well-lit area

616 You are in the right-hand lane of a dual carriageway. You see signs showing that the right lane is closed 800 yards ahead. You should

Mark one answer

- A. keep in that lane until you reach the queue
- B. move to the left immediately
- C. wait and see which lane is moving faster
- D. move to the left in good time

617 You are driving on an urban clearway. You may stop only to

Mark one answer

- A. set down and pick up passengers
- B. use a mobile telephone
- C. ask for directions
- D. load or unload goods

618 You are looking for somewhere to park your vehicle. The area is full EXCEPT for spaces marked 'disabled use'. You can

Mark one answer

- A. use these spaces when elsewhere is full
- B. park if you stay with your vehicle
- C. use these spaces, disabled or not
- D. not park there unless permitted

619 Your vehicle is parked on the road at night. When must you use sidelights?

Mark one answer

- A. Where there are continuous white lines in the middle of the road
- B. Where the speed limit exceeds 30mph
- C. Where you are facing oncoming traffic
- D. Where you are near a bus stop

620 On which THREE occasions MUST you stop your vehicle?

Mark three answers

- A. When involved in an accident
- B. At a red traffic light
- C. When signalled to do so by a police officer
- D. At a junction with double broken white lines
- E. At a pelican crossing when the amber light is flashing and no pedestrians are crossing

621 You are on a road that is only wide enough for one vehicle. There is a car coming towards you. What should you do?

Mark one answer

- A. Pull into a passing place on your right
- B. Force the other driver to reverse
- C. Pull into a passing place if your vehicle is wider
- D. Pull into a passing place on your left

622 What MUST you have to park in a disabled space?

Mark one answer

- [ ] A. An orange or blue badge
- [ ] B. A wheelchair
- [ ] C. An advanced driver certificate
- [ ] D. A modified vehicle

623 You are driving at night with full beam headlights on. A vehicle is overtaking you. You should dip your lights

Mark one answer

- [ ] A. some time after the vehicle has passed you
- [ ] B. before the vehicle starts to pass you
- [ ] C. only if the other driver dips their headlights
- [ ] D. as soon as the vehicle passes you

TIP You can recognise a car driven by someone who is disabled because they display a **Blue Card** (formerly an Orange Badge). This gives them the right to park in a space with disabilities.

624 When may you drive a motor car in this bus lane?

Mark one answer

- [ ] A. Outside its hours of operation
- [ ] B. To get to the front of a traffic queue
- [ ] C. You may not use it at any time
- [ ] D. To overtake slow-moving traffic

625 Signals are normally given by direction indicators and

Mark one answer

- [ ] A. brake lights
- [ ] B. sidelights
- [ ] C. fog lights
- [ ] D. interior lights

626 You MUST obey signs giving orders. These signs are mostly in

Mark one answer
- A. green rectangles
- B. red triangles
- C. blue rectangles
- D. red circles

627 Traffic signs giving orders are generally which shape?

Mark one answer

A.

B.

C.

D.

628 Which type of sign tells you NOT to do something?

Mark one answer

A.

B.

C.

D.

629 What does this sign mean?

Mark one answer
- A. Maximum speed limit with traffic calming
- B. Minimum speed limit with traffic calming
- C. '20 cars only' parking zone
- D. Only 20 cars allowed at any one time

630 Which sign means no motor vehicles are allowed?

Mark one answer

A.

B.

C.

D.

631 Which of these signs means no motor vehicles?

Mark one answer

A.

B.

C.

D.

632 What does this sign mean?

Mark one answer

- [ ] **A.** New speed limit 20mph
- [ ] **B.** No vehicles over 30 tonnes
- [ ] **C.** Minimum speed limit 30mph
- [ ] **D.** End of 20mph zone

633 What does this sign mean?

Mark one answer

- [ ] **A.** No overtaking
- [ ] **B.** No motor vehicles
- [ ] **C.** Clearway (no stopping)
- [ ] **D.** Cars and motorcycles only

634 What does this sign mean?

Mark one answer

- [ ] **A.** No parking
- [ ] **B.** No road markings
- [ ] **C.** No through road
- [ ] **D.** No entry

635 What does this sign mean?

Mark one answer

- [ ] **A.** Bend to the right
- [ ] **B.** Road on the right closed
- [ ] **C.** No traffic from the right
- [ ] **D.** No right turn

636 Which sign means 'no entry'?

Mark one answer

- [ ] **A.**
- [ ] **B.**
- [ ] **C.**
- [ ] **D.**

637 What does this sign mean?

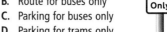

Mark one answer

- [ ] **A.** Route for trams only
- [ ] **B.** Route for buses only
- [ ] **C.** Parking for buses only
- [ ] **D.** Parking for trams only

638 Which type of vehicle does this sign apply to?

Mark one answer
- A. Wide vehicles
- B. Long vehicles
- C. High vehicles
- D. Heavy vehicles

639 Which sign means NO motor vehicles allowed?

Mark one answer
- A.
- B.
- C.
- D.

640 What does this sign mean?

Mark one answer
- A. You have priority
- B. No motor vehicles
- C. Two-way traffic
- D. No overtaking

641 What does this sign mean?

Mark one answer
- A. Keep in one lane
- B. Give way to oncoming traffic
- C. Do not overtake
- D. Form two lanes

642 Which sign means no overtaking?

Mark one answer
- A.
- B.
- C.
- D.

643 What does this sign mean?

Mark one answer
- A. Waiting restrictions apply
- B. Waiting permitted
- C. National speed limit applies
- D. Clearway (no stopping)

644 What does this sign mean?

Mark one answer
- [ ] **A.** End of restricted speed area
- [ ] **B.** End of restricted parking area
- [ ] **C.** End of clearway
- [ ] **D.** End of cycle route

645 Which sign means 'no stopping'?

Mark one answer
- [ ] **A.**
- [ ] **B.**
- [ ] **C.**
- [ ] **D.**

646 What does this sign mean?

Mark one answer
- [ ] **A.** Roundabout
- [ ] **B.** Crossroads
- [ ] **C.** No stopping
- [ ] **D.** No entry

647 You see this sign ahead. It means

Mark one answer
- [ ] **A.** national speed limit applies
- [ ] **B.** waiting restrictions apply
- [ ] **C.** no stopping
- [ ] **D.** no entry

648 What does this sign mean?

Mark one answer
- [ ] **A.** Distance to parking place ahead
- [ ] **B.** Distance to public telephone ahead
- [ ] **C.** Distance to public house ahead
- [ ] **D.** Distance to passing place ahead

649 What does this sign mean?

Mark one answer
- [ ] **A.** Vehicles may not park on the verge or footway
- [ ] **B.** Vehicles may park on the left-hand side of the road only
- [ ] **C.** Vehicles may park fully on the verge or footway
- [ ] **D.** Vehicles may park on the right-hand side of the road only

TIP Remember that where there are street lamps spaced less than 185 metres (202 yards) apart, a 30mph speed limit applies unless signs on the posts state otherwise.

650 What does this traffic sign mean?

Mark one answer

- A. No overtaking allowed
- B. Give priority to oncoming traffic
- C. Two-way traffic
- D. One-way traffic only

651 What is the meaning of this traffic sign?

Mark one answer

- A. End of two-way road
- B. Give priority to vehicles coming towards you
- C. You have priority over vehicles coming towards you
- D. Bus lane ahead

652 What MUST you do when you see this sign?

Mark one answer

- A. Stop, ONLY if traffic is approaching
- B. Stop, even if the road is clear
- C. Stop, ONLY if children are waiting to cross
- D. Stop, ONLY if a red light is showing

653 What does this sign mean?

Mark one answer

- A. No overtaking
- B. You are entering a one-way street
- C. Two-way traffic ahead
- D. You have priority over vehicles from the opposite direction

654 What shape is a STOP sign at a junction?

Mark one answer

- A.
- B.
- C.
- D.

655 At a junction you see this sign partly covered by snow. What does it mean?

Mark one answer

- A. Crossroads
- B. Give way
- C. Stop
- D. Turn right

656 Which shape is used for a GIVE WAY sign?

Mark one answer

A.

B.

C.

D.

657 What does this sign mean?

Mark one answer

A. Service area 30 miles ahead

B. Maximum speed 30mph

C. Minimum speed 30mph

D. Lay-by 30 miles ahead

658 Which of these signs means turn left ahead?

Mark one answer

A.

B.

C.

D.

659 What does this sign mean?

Mark one answer

A. Buses turning

B. Ring road

C. Mini-roundabout

D. Keep right

660 What does this sign mean?

Mark one answer

A. Give way to oncoming vehicles

B. Approaching traffic passes you on both sides

C. Turn off at the next available junction

D. Pass either side to get to the same destination

661 What does this sign mean?

Mark one answer

A. Route for trams

B. Give way to trams

C. Route for buses

D. Give way to buses

662 What does a circular traffic sign with a blue background do?

Mark one answer

- [ ] A. Give warning of a motorway ahead
- [ ] B. Give directions to a car park
- [ ] C. Give motorway information
- [ ] D. Give an instruction

663 Which of these signs means that you are entering a one-way street?

Mark one answer

- [ ] A.
- [ ] B.
- [ ] C.
- [ ] D.

664 Where would you see a contraflow bus and cycle lane?

Mark one answer

- [ ] A. On a dual carriageway
- [ ] B. On a roundabout
- [ ] C. On an urban motorway
- [ ] D. On a one-way street

665 What does this sign mean?

Mark one answer

- [ ] A. Bus station on the right
- [ ] B. Contraflow bus lane
- [ ] C. With-flow bus lane
- [ ] D. Give way to buses

666 What does this sign mean?

Mark one answer

- [ ] A. With-flow bus and cycle lane
- [ ] B. Contraflow bus and cycle lane
- [ ] C. No buses and cycles allowed
- [ ] D. No waiting for buses and cycles

667 What does a sign with a brown background show?

Mark one answer

- [ ] A. Tourist directions
- [ ] B. Primary roads
- [ ] C. Motorway routes
- [ ] D. Minor routes

668 This sign means

Mark one answer
- **A.** tourist attraction
- **B.** beware of trains
- **C.** level crossing
- **D.** beware of trams

669 What are triangular signs for?

Mark one answer
- **A.** To give warnings
- **B.** To give information
- **C.** To give orders
- **D.** To give directions

670 What does this sign mean?

Mark one answer
- **A.** Turn left ahead
- **B.** T-junction
- **C.** No through road
- **D.** Give way

671 What does this sign mean?

Mark one answer
- **A.** Multi-exit roundabout
- **B.** Risk of ice
- **C.** Six roads converge
- **D.** Place of historical interest

672 What does this sign mean?

Mark one answer
- **A.** Crossroads
- **B.** Level crossing with gate
- **C.** Level crossing without gate
- **D.** Ahead only

673 What does this sign mean?

Mark one answer
- **A.** Ring road
- **B.** Mini-roundabout
- **C.** No vehicles
- **D.** Roundabout

674 Which FOUR of these would be indicated by a triangular road sign?

Mark four answers
- A. Road narrows
- B. Ahead only
- C. Low bridge
- D. Minimum speed
- E. Children crossing
- F. T-junction

675 What does this sign mean?

Mark one answer
- A. Cyclists must dismount
- B. Cycles are not allowed
- C. Cycle route ahead
- D. Cycle in single file

676 Which sign means that pedestrians may be walking along the road?

Mark one answer
- A.
- B.
- C.
- D.

677 Which of these signs warn you of a pedestrian crossing?

Mark one answer
- A.
- B.
- C.
- D.

678 What does this sign mean?

Mark one answer
- A. No footpath ahead
- B. Pedestrians only ahead
- C. Pedestrian crossing ahead
- D. School crossing ahead

679 What does this sign mean?

Mark one answer
- A. School crossing patrol
- B. No pedestrians allowed
- C. Pedestrian zone -- no vehicles
- D. Pedestrian crossing ahead

680 Which of these signs means there is a double bend ahead?

Mark one answer

A.

B.

C.

D.

681 What does this sign mean?

Mark one answer

A. Wait at the barriers
B. Wait at the crossroads
C. Give way to trams
D. Give way to farm vehicles

682 What does this sign mean?

Mark one answer

A. Humpback bridge
B. Humps in the road
C. Entrance to tunnel
D. Soft verges

683 What does this sign mean?

Mark one answer

A. Low bridge ahead
B. Tunnel ahead
C. Ancient monument ahead
D. Accident black spot ahead

684 What does this sign mean?

Mark one answer

A. Two-way traffic straight ahead
B. Two-way traffic crossing a one-way street
C. Two-way traffic over a bridge
D. Two-way traffic crosses a two-way road

685 Which sign means 'two-way traffic crosses a one-way road'?

Mark one answer

A.

B.

C.

D.

686 Which of these signs means the end of a dual carriageway?

Mark one answer

A.

B.

C.

D.

687 What does this sign mean?

Mark one answer

A. End of dual carriageway
B. Tall bridge
C. Road narrows
D. End of narrow bridge

688 What does this sign mean?

Mark one answer

A. Two-way traffic ahead across a one-way street
B. Traffic approaching you has priority
C. Two-way traffic straight ahead
D. Motorway contraflow system ahead

689 What does this sign mean?

Mark one answer

A. Crosswinds
B. Road noise
C. Airport
D. Adverse camber

690 What does this traffic sign mean?

Mark one answer

A. Slippery road ahead
B. Tyres liable to punctures ahead
C. Danger ahead
D. Service area ahead

691 You are about to overtake when you see this sign. You should

Mark one answer

A. overtake the other driver as quickly as possible
B. move to the right to get a better view
C. switch your headlights on before overtaking
D. hold back until you can see clearly ahead

Hidden dip

692 What does this sign mean?

Mark one answer
- [ ] **A.** Level crossing with gate or barrier
- [ ] **B.** Gated road ahead
- [ ] **C.** Level crossing without gate or barrier
- [ ] **D.** Cattle grid ahead

693 What does this sign mean?

Mark one answer
- [ ] **A.** No trams ahead
- [ ] **B.** Oncoming trams
- [ ] **C.** Trams crossing ahead
- [ ] **D.** Trams only

694 What does this sign mean?

Mark one answer
- [ ] **A.** Adverse camber
- [ ] **B.** Steep hill downwards
- [ ] **C.** Uneven road
- [ ] **D.** Steep hill upwards

695 What does this sign mean?

Mark one answer
- [ ] **A.** Uneven road surface
- [ ] **B.** Bridge over the road
- [ ] **C.** Road ahead ends
- [ ] **D.** Water across the road

696 What does this sign mean?

Mark one answer
- [ ] **A.** Humpback bridge
- [ ] **B.** Traffic calming hump
- [ ] **C.** Low bridge
- [ ] **D.** Uneven road

697 What does this sign mean?

Mark one answer
- [ ] **A.** Turn left for parking area
- [ ] **B.** No through road on the left
- [ ] **C.** No entry for traffic turning left
- [ ] **D.** Turn left for ferry terminal

698 What does this sign mean?

Mark one answer
- A. T-junction
- B. No through road
- C. Telephone box ahead
- D. Toilet ahead

699 Which sign means 'no through road'?

Mark one answer

A.

B.

C.

D.

700 Which of the following signs informs you that you are coming to a No Through Road?

Mark one answer

A.

B.

C.

D.

701 What does this sign mean?

Mark one answer
- A. Direction to park and ride car park
- B. No parking for buses or coaches
- C. Directions to bus and coach park
- D. Parking area for cars and coaches

702 You are driving through a tunnel and you see this sign. What does it mean?

Mark one answer
- A. Direction to emergency pedestrian exit
- B. Beware of pedestrians, no footpath ahead
- C. No access for pedestrians
- D. Beware of pedestrians crossing ahead

703 Which is the sign for a ring road?

Mark one answer

A.

B.

C.

D.

704 What does this sign mean?

Mark one answer

- **A.** Route for lorries
- **B.** Ring road
- **C.** Rest area
- **D.** Roundabout

705 What does this sign mean?

Mark one answer

- **A.** Hilly road
- **B.** Humps in road
- **C.** Holiday route
- **D.** Hospital route

706 What does this sign mean?

Mark one answer

- **A.** The right-hand lane ahead is narrow
- **B.** Right-hand lane for buses only
- **C.** Right-hand lane for turning right
- **D.** The right-hand lane is closed

707 What does this sign mean?

Mark one answer

- **A.** Change to the left lane
- **B.** Leave at the next exit
- **C.** Contraflow system
- **D.** One-way street

708 To avoid an accident when entering a contraflow system, you should

Mark three answers

- **A.** reduce speed in good time
- **B.** switch lanes any time to make progress
- **C.** choose an appropriate lane early
- **D.** keep the correct separation distance
- **E.** increase speed to pass through quickly
- **F.** follow other motorists closely to avoid long queues

709 What does this sign mean?

Mark one answer

- **A.** Leave motorway at next exit
- **B.** Lane for heavy and slow vehicles
- **C.** All lorries use the hard shoulder
- **D.** Rest area for lorries

710
You are approaching a red traffic light. The signal will change from red to

Mark one answer
- A. red and amber, then green
- B. green, then amber
- C. amber, then green
- D. green and amber, then green

711
A red traffic light means

Mark one answer
- A. you should stop unless turning left
- B. stop, if you are able to brake safely
- C. you must stop and wait behind the stop line
- D. proceed with caution

712
At traffic lights, amber on its own means

Mark one answer
- A. prepare to go
- B. go if the way is clear
- C. go if no pedestrians are crossing
- D. stop at the stop line

713
You are approaching traffic lights. Red and amber are showing. This means

Mark one answer
- A. pass the lights if the road is clear
- B. there is a fault with the lights – take care
- C. wait for the green light before you pass the lights
- D. the lights are about to change to red

714
You are at a junction controlled by traffic lights. When should you NOT proceed at green?

Mark one answer
- A. When pedestrians are waiting to cross
- B. When your exit from the junction is blocked
- C. When you think the lights may be about to change
- D. When you intend to turn right

715
You are in the left-hand lane at traffic lights. You are waiting to turn left. At which of these traffic lights must you NOT move on?

Mark one answer
- A.
- B.
- C.
- D.

716 What does this sign mean?

Mark one answer
- A. Traffic lights out of order
- B. Amber signal out of order
- C. Temporary traffic lights ahead
- D. New traffic lights ahead

717 When traffic lights are out of order, who has priority?

Mark one answer
- A. Traffic going straight on
- B. Traffic turning right
- C. Nobody
- D. Traffic turning left

718 These flashing red lights mean STOP. In which THREE of the following places could you find them?

Mark three answers
- A. Pelican crossings
- B. Lifting bridges
- C. Zebra crossings
- D. Level crossings
- E. Motorway exits
- F. Fire stations

719 What do these zigzag lines at pedestrian crossings mean?

Mark one answer
- A. No parking at any time
- B. Parking allowed only for a short time
- C. Slow down to 20mph
- D. Sounding horns is not allowed

720 When may you cross a double solid white line in the middle of the road?

Mark one answer
- A. To pass traffic that is queuing back at a junction
- B. To pass a car signalling to turn left ahead
- C. To pass a road maintenance vehicle travelling at 10mph or less
- D. To pass a vehicle that is towing a trailer

721 What does this road marking mean?

Mark one answer

- **A.** Do not cross the line
- **B.** No stopping allowed
- **C.** You are approaching a hazard
- **D.** No overtaking allowed

722 This marking appears on the road just before a

Mark one answer

- **A.** no entry sign
- **B.** give way sign
- **C.** stop sign
- **D.** no through road sign

723 Where would you see this road marking?

Mark one answer

- **A.** At traffic lights
- **B.** On road humps
- **C.** Near a level crossing
- **D.** At a box junction

724 Which is a hazard warning line?

Mark one answer

- **A.**

- **B.**

- **C.**

- **D.**

725 At this junction there is a stop sign with a solid white line on the road surface. Why is there a stop sign here?

Mark one answer

- **A.** Speed on the major road is de-restricted
- **B.** It is a busy junction
- **C.** Visibility along the major road is restricted
- **D.** There are hazard warning lines in the centre of the road

726 You see this line across the road at the entrance to a roundabout. What does it mean?

Mark one answer

- [ ] **A.** Give way to traffic from the right
- [ ] **B.** Traffic from the left has right of way
- [ ] **C.** You have right of way
- [ ] **D.** Stop at the line

727 Where would you find this road marking?

Mark one answer

- [ ] **A.** At a railway crossing
- [ ] **B.** At a junction
- [ ] **C.** On a motorway
- [ ] **D.** On a pedestrian crossing

728 How will a police officer in a patrol vehicle normally get you to stop?

Mark one answer

- [ ] **A.** Flash the headlights, indicate left and point to the left
- [ ] **B.** Wait until you stop, then approach you
- [ ] **C.** Use the siren, overtake, cut in front and stop
- [ ] **D.** Pull alongside you, use the siren and wave you to stop

729 There is a police car following you. The police officer flashes the headlights and points to the left. What should you do?

Mark one answer

- [ ] **A.** Turn at the next left
- [ ] **B.** Pull up on the left
- [ ] **C.** Stop immediately
- [ ] **D.** Move over to the left

730 You approach a junction. The traffic lights are not working. A police officer gives this signal. You should

Mark one answer

- [ ] **A.** turn left only
- [ ] **B.** turn right only
- [ ] **C.** stop level with the officer's arm
- [ ] **D.** stop at the stop line

731 The driver of the car in front is giving this arm signal. What does it mean?

Mark one answer

- [ ] **A.** The driver is slowing down
- [ ] **B.** The driver intends to turn right
- [ ] **C.** The driver wishes to overtake
- [ ] **D.** The driver intends to turn left

732 Where would you see these road markings?

Mark one answer
- [ ] **A.** At a level crossing
- [ ] **B.** On a motorway slip road
- [ ] **C.** At a pedestrian crossing
- [ ] **D.** On a single-track road

733 When may you NOT overtake on the left?

Mark one answer
- [ ] **A.** On a free-flowing motorway or dual carriageway
- [ ] **B.** When the traffic is moving slowly in queues
- [ ] **C.** On a one-way street
- [ ] **D.** When the car in front is signalling to turn right

734 What does this motorway sign mean?

Mark one answer
- [ ] **A.** Change to the lane on your left
- [ ] **B.** Leave the motorway at the next exit
- [ ] **C.** Change to the opposite carriageway
- [ ] **D.** Pull up on the hard shoulder

735 What does this motorway sign mean?

Mark one answer
- [ ] **A.** Temporary minimum speed 50mph
- [ ] **B.** No services for 50 miles
- [ ] **C.** Obstruction 50 metres (164 feet) ahead
- [ ] **D.** Temporary maximum speed 50mph

736 What does this sign mean?

Mark one answer
- [ ] **A.** Through traffic to use left lane
- [ ] **B.** Right-hand lane T-junction only
- [ ] **C.** Right-hand lane closed ahead
- [ ] **D.** 11 tonne weight limit

737 On a motorway this sign means

Mark one answer
- [ ] **A.** move over on to the hard shoulder
- [ ] **B.** overtaking on the left only
- [ ] **C.** leave the motorway at the next exit
- [ ] **D.** move to the lane on your left

738 What does '25' mean on this motorway sign?

Mark one answer

- [ ] **A.** The distance to the nearest town
- [ ] **B.** The route number of the road
- [ ] **C.** The number of the next junction
- [ ] **D.** The speed limit on the slip road

739 The right-hand lane of a three-lane motorway is

Mark one answer

- [ ] **A.** for lorries only
- [ ] **B.** an overtaking lane
- [ ] **C.** the right-turn lane
- [ ] **D.** an acceleration lane

740 Where can you find reflective amber studs on a motorway?

Mark one answer

- [ ] **A.** Separating the slip road from the motorway
- [ ] **B.** On the left-hand edge of the road
- [ ] **C.** On the right-hand edge of the road
- [ ] **D.** Separating the lanes

741 Where on a motorway would you find green reflective studs?

Mark one answer

- [ ] **A.** Separating driving lanes
- [ ] **B.** Between the hard shoulder and the carriageway
- [ ] **C.** At slip road entrances and exits
- [ ] **D.** Between the carriageway and the central reservation

742 You are travelling along a motorway. You see this sign. You should

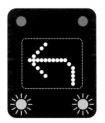

Mark one answer

- [ ] **A.** leave the motorway at the next exit
- [ ] **B.** turn left immediately
- [ ] **C.** change lane
- [ ] **D.** move on to the hard shoulder

743 What does this sign mean?

Mark one answer

- [ ] **A.** No motor vehicles
- [ ] **B.** End of motorway
- [ ] **C.** No through road
- [ ] **D.** End of bus lane

Section 11 – Road and Traffic Signs

744 Which of these signs means that the national speed limit applies?

Mark one answer
- [ ] A.
- [ ] B.
- [ ] C.
- [ ] D.

745 What is the maximum speed on a single carriageway road?

Mark one answer
- [ ] A. 50mph
- [ ] B. 60mph
- [ ] C. 40mph
- [ ] D. 70mph

746 What does this sign mean?

Mark one answer
- [ ] A. End of motorway
- [ ] B. End of restriction
- [ ] C. Lane ends ahead
- [ ] D. Free recovery ends

747 This sign is advising you to

Mark one answer
- [ ] A. follow the route diversion
- [ ] B. follow the signs to the picnic area
- [ ] C. give way to pedestrians
- [ ] D. give way to cyclists

748 Why would this temporary speed limit sign be shown?

Mark one answer
- [ ] A. To warn of the end of the motorway
- [ ] B. To warn you of a low bridge
- [ ] C. To warn you of a junction ahead
- [ ] D. To warn of road works ahead

749 This traffic sign means there is

Mark one answer
- [ ] A. a compulsory maximum speed limit
- [ ] B. an advisory maximum speed limit
- [ ] C. a compulsory minimum speed limit
- [ ] D. an advised separation distance

750 You see this sign at a crossroads. You should

Mark one answer

- [ ] A. maintain the same speed
- [ ] B. carry on with great care
- [ ] C. find another route
- [ ] D. telephone the police

751 You are signalling to turn right in busy traffic. How would you confirm your intention safely?

Mark one answer

- [ ] A. Sound the horn
- [ ] B. Give an arm signal
- [ ] C. Flash your headlights
- [ ] D. Position over the centre line

752 What does this sign mean?

Mark one answer

- [ ] A. Motorcycles only
- [ ] B. No cars
- [ ] C. Cars only
- [ ] D. No motorcycles

753 You are on a motorway. You see this sign on a lorry that has stopped in the right-hand lane. You should

Mark one answer

- [ ] A. move into the right-hand lane
- [ ] B. stop behind the flashing lights
- [ ] C. pass the lorry on the left
- [ ] D. leave the motorway at the next exit

754 You are on a motorway. Red flashing lights appear above your lane only. What should you do?

Mark one answer

- [ ] A. Continue in that lane and look for further information
- [ ] B. Move into another lane in good time
- [ ] C. Pull on to the hard shoulder
- [ ] D. Stop and wait for an instruction to proceed

755 A red traffic light means

Mark one answer

- [ ] A. you must stop behind the white stop line
- [ ] B. you may go straight on if there is no other traffic
- [ ] C. you may turn left if it is safe to do so
- [ ] D. you must slow down and prepare to stop if traffic has started to cross

756
The driver of this car is giving an arm signal. What are they about to do?

Mark one answer
- A. Turn to the right
- B. Turn to the left
- C. Go straight ahead
- D. Let pedestrians cross

757
Which arm signal tells you that the car you are following is going to turn left?

Mark one answer

A. 　　　B.

C. 　　　D.

758
When may you sound the horn?

Mark one answer
- A. To give you right of way
- B. To attract a friend's attention
- C. To warn others of your presence
- D. To make slower drivers move over

759
You must not use your horn when you are stationary

Mark one answer
- A. unless a moving vehicle may cause you danger
- B. at any time whatsoever
- C. unless it is used only briefly
- D. except for signalling that you have just arrived

760
What does this sign mean?

Mark one answer
- A. You can park on the days and times shown
- B. No parking on the days and times shown
- C. No parking at all from Monday to Friday
- D. End of the urban clearway restrictions

761
What does this sign mean?

Mark one answer
- A. Quayside or river bank
- B. Steep hill downwards
- C. Uneven road surface
- D. Road liable to flooding

762 You see this amber traffic light ahead. Which light(s) will come on next?

Mark one answer
- [ ] **A.** Red alone
- [ ] **B.** Red and amber together
- [ ] **C.** Green and amber together
- [ ] **D.** Green alone

763 The white line painted in the centre of the road means

Mark one answer
- [ ] **A.** oncoming vehicles have priority over you
- [ ] **B.** you should give priority to oncoming vehicles
- [ ] **C.** there is a hazard ahead of you
- [ ] **D.** the area is a national speed limit zone

764 Which sign means you have priority over oncoming vehicles?

Mark one answer
- [ ] **A.**
- [ ] **B.**
- [ ] **C.**
- [ ] **D.**

765 You see this signal overhead on the motorway. What does it mean?

Mark one answer
- [ ] **A.** Leave the motorway at the next exit
- [ ] **B.** All vehicles use the hard shoulder
- [ ] **C.** Sharp bend to the left ahead
- [ ] **D.** Stop, all lanes ahead closed

766 A white line like this along the centre of the road is a

Mark one answer
- [ ] **A.** bus lane marking
- [ ] **B.** hazard warning
- [ ] **C.** give way marking
- [ ] **D.** lane marking

> **TIP** The outside lane of a motorway can't be used by vehicles weighing over 7.5 tonnes, and passenger vehicles over 7.5 tonnes or over 12 metres in length, or adapted to carry more than 8 passengers.

767 What is the purpose of these yellow criss-cross lines on the road?

Mark one answer

- **A.** To make you more aware of the traffic lights
- **B.** To guide you into position as you turn
- **C.** To prevent the junction from becoming blocked
- **D.** To show you where to stop when the lights change

768 What is the reason for the yellow criss-cross lines painted on the road here?

Mark one answer

- **A.** To mark out an area for trams only
- **B.** To prevent queuing traffic from blocking the junction on the left
- **C.** To mark the entrance lane to a car park
- **D.** To warn you of the tram lines crossing the road

769 What is the reason for the area marked in red and white along the centre of this road?

Mark one answer

- **A.** It is to separate traffic flowing in opposite directions
- **B.** It marks an area to be used by overtaking motorcyclists
- **C.** It is a temporary marking to warn of the road works
- **D.** It is separating the two sides of the dual carriageway

770 Other drivers may sometimes flash their headlights at you. In which situation are they allowed to do this?

Mark one answer

- **A.** To warn of a radar speed trap ahead
- **B.** To show that they are giving way to you
- **C.** To warn you of their presence
- **D.** To let you know there is a fault with your vehicle

771 At road works which of the following can control traffic flow?

Mark three answers

- **A.** A STOP–GO board
- **B.** Flashing amber lights
- **C.** A police officer
- **D.** Flashing red lights
- **E.** Temporary traffic lights

772

You are approaching a zebra crossing where pedestrians are waiting. Which arm signal might you give?

Mark one answer

A.

B.

C.

D.

773

The white line along the side of the road

Mark one answer

A. shows the edge of the carriageway
B. shows the approach to a hazard
C. means no parking
D. means no overtaking

774

You see this white arrow on the road ahead. It means

Mark one answer

A. entrance on the left
B. all vehicles turn left
C. keep left of the hatched markings
D. road bending to the left

775

How should you give an arm signal to turn left?

Mark one answer

A.

B.

C.

D.

776

You are waiting at a T-junction. A vehicle is coming from the right with the left signal flashing. What should you do?

Mark one answer

A. Move out and accelerate hard
B. Wait until the vehicle starts to turn in
C. Pull out before the vehicle reaches the junction
D. Move out slowly

777 When may you use hazard warning lights when driving?

Mark one answer

- [ ] A. Instead of sounding the horn in a built-up area between 11.30pm and 7am
- [ ] B. On a motorway or unrestricted dual carriageway, to warn of a hazard ahead
- [ ] C. On rural routes, after a warning sign of animals
- [ ] D. On the approach to toucan crossings where cyclists are waiting to cross

778 You are driving on a motorway. There is a slow-moving vehicle ahead. On the back you see this sign. You should

Mark one answer

- [ ] A. pass on the right
- [ ] B. pass on the left
- [ ] C. leave at the next exit
- [ ] D. drive no further

TIP *The Highway Code* states that the only reason for flashing your lights is **to let others know you are there**. Many people flash their lights to indicate they are **letting another motorist go first**. But in general, you should not assume it is safe to proceed on the basis of such a signal – the lights may not be flashed at you but at someone else.

779 You should NOT normally stop on these markings near schools

SCHOOL KEEP CLEAR

Mark one answer

- [ ] A. except when picking up children
- [ ] B. under any circumstances
- [ ] C. unless there is nowhere else available
- [ ] D. except to set down children

780 Why should you make sure that your indicators are cancelled after turning?

Mark one answer

- [ ] A. To avoid flattening the battery
- [ ] B. To avoid misleading other road users
- [ ] C. To avoid dazzling other road users
- [ ] D. To avoid damage to the indicator relay

781 You are driving in busy traffic. You want to pull up on the left just after a junction on the left. When should you signal?

Mark one answer

- [ ] A. As you are passing or just after the junction
- [ ] B. Just before you reach the junction
- [ ] C. Well before you reach the junction
- [ ] D. It would be better not to signal at all

782 An MOT certificate is normally valid for

Mark one answer

- A. three years after the date it was issued
- B. 10,000 miles
- C. one year after the date it was issued
- D. 30,000 miles

783 A cover note is a document issued before you receive your

Mark one answer

- A. driving licence
- B. insurance certificate
- C. registration document
- D. MOT certificate

784 A police officer asks to see your documents. You do not have them with you. You may produce them at a police station within

Mark one answer **NI**

- A. five days
- B. seven days
- C. 14 days
- D. 21 days

785 You have just passed your practical test. You do not hold a full licence in another category. Within two years you get six penalty points on your licence. What will you have to do?

Mark two answers

- A. Retake only your theory test
- B. Retake your theory and practical tests
- C. Retake only your practical test
- D. Reapply for your full licence immediately
- E. Reapply for your provisional licence

786 To drive on the road learners MUST

Mark one answer

- A. have NO penalty points on their licence
- B. have taken professional instruction
- C. have a signed, valid provisional licence
- D. apply for a driving test within 12 months

787 Before driving anyone else's motor vehicle you should make sure that

Mark one answer

- A. the vehicle owner has third party insurance cover
- B. your own vehicle has insurance cover
- C. the vehicle is insured for your use
- D. the owner has left the insurance documents in the vehicle

788 Your car needs an MOT certificate. If you drive without one this could invalidate your

Mark one answer

- A. vehicle service record
- B. insurance
- C. road tax disc
- D. vehicle registration document

TIP Remember, a fine for speeding leads to penalty points on your licence. If you accumulate six penalty points within two years of passing your test, your licence will be revoked.

789 When is it legal to drive a car over three years old without an MOT certificate?

Mark one answer **NI**

- A. Up to seven days after the old certificate has run out
- B. When driving to an MOT centre to arrange an appointment
- C. Just after buying a second-hand car with no MOT
- D. When driving to an appointment at an MOT centre

790 To supervise a learner driver you must

Mark two answers

- A. have held a full licence for at least 3 years
- B. be at least 21
- C. be an approved driving instructor
- D. hold an advanced driving certificate

791 The cost of your insurance may be reduced if

Mark one answer

- A. your car is large and powerful
- B. you are using the car for work purposes
- C. you have penalty points on your licence
- D. you are over 25 years old

792 How old must you be to supervise a learner driver?

Mark one answer

- A. 18 years old
- B. 19 years old
- C. 20 years old
- D. 21 years old

793 A newly qualified driver must

Mark one answer

- A. display green 'L' plates
- B. not exceed 40mph for 12 months
- C. be accompanied on a motorway
- D. have valid motor insurance

794 What is the legal minimum insurance cover you must have to drive on public roads?

Mark one answer

- A. Third party, fire and theft
- B. Fully comprehensive
- C. Third party only
- D. Personal Injury cover

795 You have third party insurance. What does this cover?

Mark three answers

- A. Damage to your own vehicle
- B. Damage to your vehicle by fire
- C. Injury to another person
- D. Damage to someone's property
- E. Damage to other vehicles
- F. Injury to yourself

796 For which TWO of these must you show your motor insurance certificate?

Mark two answers

- A. When you are taking your driving test
- B. When buying or selling a vehicle
- C. When a police officer asks you for it
- D. When you are taxing your vehicle
- E. When having an MOT inspection

797 Vehicle excise duty is often called 'Road Tax' or 'The Tax Disc'. You must

Mark one answer

- [ ] A. keep it with your registration document
- [ ] B. display it clearly on your vehicle
- [ ] C. keep it concealed safely in your vehicle
- [ ] D. carry it on you at all times

798 Motor cars must FIRST have an MOT test certificate when they are

Mark one answer **NI**

- [ ] A. one year old
- [ ] B. three years old
- [ ] C. five years old
- [ ] D. seven years old

799 Your vehicle needs a current MOT certificate. You do not have one. Until you do have one you will not be able to renew your

Mark one answer

- [ ] A. driving licence
- [ ] B. vehicle insurance
- [ ] C. road tax disc
- [ ] D. vehicle registration document

800 Which THREE pieces of information are found on a vehicle registration document?

Mark three answers

- [ ] A. Registered keeper
- [ ] B. Make of the vehicle
- [ ] C. Service history details
- [ ] D. Date of the MOT
- [ ] E. Type of insurance cover
- [ ] F. Engine size

801 You have a duty to contact the licensing authority when

Mark three answers

- [ ] A. you go abroad on holiday
- [ ] B. you change your vehicle
- [ ] C. you change your name
- [ ] D. your job status is changed
- [ ] E. your permanent address changes
- [ ] F. your job involves travelling abroad

802 You must notify the licensing authority when

Mark three answers

- [ ] A. your health affects your driving
- [ ] B. your eyesight does not meet a set standard
- [ ] C. you intend lending your vehicle
- [ ] D. your vehicle requires an MOT certificate
- [ ] E. you change your vehicle

803 You have just bought a second-hand vehicle. When should you tell the licensing authority of change of ownership?

Mark one answer

- [ ] A. Immediately
- [ ] B. After 28 days
- [ ] C. When an MOT is due
- [ ] D. Only when you insure it

804 Your vehicle is insured third party only. This covers

Mark two answers

- [ ] A. damage to your vehicle
- [ ] B. damage to other vehicles
- [ ] C. injury to yourself
- [ ] D. injury to others
- [ ] E. all damage and injury

805 Your motor insurance policy has an excess of £100. What does this mean?

Mark one answer

- [ ] A. The insurance company will pay the first £100 of any claim
- [ ] B. You will be paid £100 if you do not have an accident
- [ ] C. Your vehicle is insured for a value of £100 if it is stolen
- [ ] D. You will have to pay the first £100 of any claim

806 When you apply to renew your vehicle excise licence (tax disc) you must produce

Mark one answer

- [ ] A. a valid insurance certificate
- [ ] B. the old tax disc
- [ ] C. the vehicle handbook
- [ ] D. a valid driving licence

807 What is the legal minimum insurance cover you must have to drive on public roads?

Mark one answer

- [ ] A. Fire and theft
- [ ] B. Theft only
- [ ] C. Third party
- [ ] D. Fire only

AA Car Insurance will find you the lowest quote they can from their panel of leading insurers.
Call 0800 032 3846 quoting ref: 860

808 Which THREE of the following do you need before you can drive legally?

Mark three answers

- [ ] A. A valid driving licence with signature
- [ ] B. A valid tax disc displayed on your vehicle
- [ ] C. A vehicle service record
- [ ] D. Proper insurance cover
- [ ] E. Breakdown cover
- [ ] F. A vehicle handbook

809 The cost of your insurance may reduce if you

NI

Mark one answer

- [ ] A. are under 25 years old
- [ ] B. do not wear glasses
- [ ] C. pass the driving test first time
- [ ] D. take the Pass Plus scheme

810 Which of the following may reduce the cost of your insurance?

NI

Mark one answer

- [ ] A. Having a valid MOT certificate
- [ ] B. Taking a Pass Plus course
- [ ] C. Driving a powerful car
- [ ] D. Having penalty points on your licence

811 The Pass Plus scheme has been created for new drivers. What is its main purpose?

NI

Mark one answer

- [ ] A. To allow you to drive faster
- [ ] B. To allow you to carry passengers
- [ ] C. To improve your basic skills
- [ ] D. To let you drive on motorways

812 At the scene of an accident you should

Mark one answer

- A. not put yourself at risk
- B. go to those casualties who are screaming
- C. pull everybody out of their vehicles
- D. leave vehicle engines switched on

813 You are the first to arrive at the scene of an accident. Which FOUR of these should you do?

Mark four answers

- A. Leave as soon as another motorist arrives
- B. Switch off the vehicle engine(s)
- C. Move uninjured people away from the vehicle(s)
- D. Call the emergency services
- E. Warn other traffic

814 An accident has just happened. An injured person is lying in the busy road. What is the FIRST thing you should do to help?

Mark one answer

- A. Treat the person for shock
- B. Warn other traffic
- C. Place them in the recovery position
- D. Make sure the injured person is kept warm

TIP At the scene of an accident remain calm and assess the situation. Ensure safety at the scene by controlling the traffic and checking that engines are switched off.

815 You are the first person to arrive at an accident where people are badly injured. Which THREE should you do?

Mark three answers

- A. Switch on your own hazard warning lights
- B. Make sure that someone telephones for an ambulance
- C. Try and get people who are injured to drink something
- D. Move the people who are injured clear of their vehicles
- E. Get people who are not injured clear of the scene

816 You arrive at the scene of a motorcycle accident. The rider is injured. When should the helmet be removed?

Mark one answer

- A. Only when it is essential
- B. Always straight away
- C. Only when the motorcyclist asks
- D. Always, unless they are in shock

817 You arrive at a serious motorcycle accident. The motorcyclist is unconscious and bleeding. Your main priorities should be to

Mark three answers

- A. try to stop the bleeding
- B. make a list of witnesses
- C. check the casualty's breathing
- D. take the numbers of the vehicles involved
- E. sweep up any loose debris
- F. check the casualty's airways

818 You arrive at an accident. A motorcyclist is unconscious. Your FIRST priority is the casualty's

Mark one answer

- A. breathing
- B. bleeding
- C. broken bones
- D. bruising

819 At an accident a casualty is unconscious. Which THREE of the following should you check urgently?

Mark three answers

- A. Circulation
- B. Airway
- C. Shock
- D. Breathing
- E. Broken bones

820 You arrive at the scene of an accident. It has just happened and someone is unconscious. Which of the following should be given urgent priority to help them?

Mark three answers

- A. Clear the airway and keep it open
- B. Try to get them to drink water
- C. Check that they are breathing
- D. Look for any witnesses
- E. Stop any heavy bleeding
- F. Take the numbers of vehicles involved

821 At an accident someone is unconscious. Your main priorities should be to

Mark three answers

- A. sweep up the broken glass
- B. take the names of witnesses
- C. count the number of vehicles involved
- D. check the airway is clear
- E. make sure they are breathing
- F. stop any heavy bleeding

822 You have stopped at the scene of an accident to give help. Which THREE things should you do?

Mark three answers

- A. Keep injured people warm and comfortable
- B. Keep injured people calm by talking to them reassuringly
- C. Keep injured people on the move by walking them around
- D. Give injured people a warm drink
- E. Make sure that injured people are not left alone

823 You arrive at the scene of an accident. It has just happened and someone is injured. Which THREE of the following should be given urgent priority?

Mark three answers

- A. Stop any severe bleeding
- B. Get them a warm drink
- C. Check that their breathing is OK
- D. Take numbers of vehicles involved
- E. Look for witnesses
- F. Clear their airway and keep it open

824 At an accident a casualty has stopped breathing. You should

Mark two answers

- [ ] A. remove anything that is blocking the mouth
- [ ] B. keep the head tilted forwards as far as possible
- [ ] C. raise the legs to help with circulation
- [ ] D. try to give the casualty something to drink
- [ ] E. keep the head tilted back as far as possible

825 You are at the scene of an accident. Someone is suffering from shock. You should

Mark four answers

- [ ] A. reassure them constantly
- [ ] B. offer them a cigarette
- [ ] C. keep them warm
- [ ] D. avoid moving them if possible
- [ ] E. loosen any tight clothing
- [ ] F. give them a warm drink

826 Which of the following should you NOT do at the scene of an accident?

Mark one answer

- [ ] A. Warn other traffic by switching on your hazard warning lights
- [ ] B. Call the emergency services immediately
- [ ] C. Offer someone a cigarette to calm them down
- [ ] D. Ask drivers to switch off their engines

827 There has been an accident. The driver is suffering from shock. You should

Mark two answers

- [ ] A. give them a drink
- [ ] B. reassure them
- [ ] C. not leave them alone
- [ ] D. offer them a cigarette
- [ ] E. ask who caused the accident

828 You are at the scene of an accident. Someone is suffering from shock. You should

Mark three answers

- [ ] A. offer them a cigarette
- [ ] B. offer them a warm drink
- [ ] C. keep them warm
- [ ] D. loosen any tight clothing
- [ ] E. reassure them constantly

829 You have to treat someone for shock at the scene of an accident. You should

Mark one answer

- [ ] A. reassure them constantly
- [ ] B. walk them around to calm them down
- [ ] C. give them something cold to drink
- [ ] D. cool them down as soon as possible

830 You arrive at the scene of a motorcycle accident. No other vehicle is involved. The rider is unconscious, lying in the middle of the road. The first thing you should do is

Mark one answer
- A. move the rider out of the road
- B. warn other traffic
- C. clear the road of debris
- D. give the rider reassurance

831 At an accident a small child is not breathing. When giving mouth to mouth you should breathe

Mark one answer
- A. sharply
- B. gently
- C. heavily
- D. rapidly

832 To start mouth to mouth on a casualty you should

Mark three answers
- A. tilt their head forward
- B. clear the airway
- C. turn them on their side
- D. tilt their head back
- E. pinch the nostrils together
- F. put their arms across their chest

833 When you are giving mouth to mouth you should only stop when

Mark one answer
- A. you think the casualty is dead
- B. the casualty can breathe without help
- C. the casualty has turned blue
- D. you think the ambulance is coming

834 You arrive at the scene of an accident. There has been an engine fire and someone's hands and arms have been burnt. You should NOT

Mark one answer
- A. douse the burn thoroughly with cool liquid
- B. lay the casualty down
- C. remove anything sticking to the burn
- D. reassure them constantly

835 You arrive at an accident where someone is suffering from severe burns. You should

Mark one answer
- A. apply lotions to the injury
- B. burst any blisters
- C. remove anything stuck to the burns
- D. douse the burns with cool liquid

836 You arrive at the scene of an accident. A pedestrian has a severe bleeding wound on their leg, although it is not broken. What should you do?

Mark two answers
- A. Dab the wound to stop bleeding
- B. Keep both legs flat on the ground
- C. Apply firm pressure to the wound
- D. Raise the leg to lessen bleeding
- E. Fetch them a warm drink

TIP Remember the **ABC** of First Aid:
A is for Airway
B is for Breathing
C is for Circulation

837 You arrive at the scene of an accident. A passenger is bleeding badly from an arm wound. What should you do?

Mark one answer

- [ ] **A.** Apply pressure over the wound and keep the arm down
- [ ] **B.** Dab the wound
- [ ] **C.** Get them a drink
- [ ] **D.** Apply pressure over the wound and raise the arm

838 You arrive at the scene of an accident. A pedestrian is bleeding heavily from a leg wound but the leg is not broken. What should you do?

Mark one answer

- [ ] **A.** Dab the wound to stop the bleeding
- [ ] **B.** Keep both legs flat on the ground
- [ ] **C.** Apply firm pressure to the wound
- [ ] **D.** Fetch them a warm drink

839 At an accident a casualty is unconscious but still breathing. You should only move them if

Mark one answer

- [ ] **A.** an ambulance is on its way
- [ ] **B.** bystanders advise you to
- [ ] **C.** there is further danger
- [ ] **D.** bystanders will help you to

840 At an accident you suspect a casualty has back injuries. The area is safe. You should

Mark one answer

- [ ] **A.** offer them a drink
- [ ] **B.** not move them
- [ ] **C.** raise their legs
- [ ] **D.** offer them a cigarette

841 At an accident it is important to look after the casualty. When the area is safe, you should

Mark one answer

- [ ] **A.** get them out of the vehicle
- [ ] **B.** give them a drink
- [ ] **C.** give them something to eat
- [ ] **D.** keep them in the vehicle

842 A tanker is involved in an accident. Which sign would show that the tanker is carrying dangerous goods?

Mark one answer

- [ ] **A.** LONG VEHICLE
- [ ] **B.** 2YE 1089

- [ ] **C.**
- [ ] **D.**

843 The police may ask you to produce which three of these documents following an accident?

Mark three answers
- [ ] **A.** Vehicle registration document
- [ ] **B.** Driving licence
- [ ] **C.** Theory test certificate
- [ ] **D.** Insurance certificate
- [ ] **E.** MOT test certificate
- [ ] **F.** Road tax disc

844 At a railway level crossing the red light signal continues to flash after a train has gone by. What should you do?

Mark one answer
- [ ] **A.** Phone the signal operator
- [ ] **B.** Alert drivers behind you
- [ ] **C.** Wait
- [ ] **D.** Proceed with caution

845 You see a car on the hard shoulder of a motorway with a HELP pennant displayed. This means the driver is most likely to be

Mark one answer
- [ ] **A.** a disabled person
- [ ] **B.** first aid trained
- [ ] **C.** a foreign visitor
- [ ] **D.** a rescue patrol person

846 On the motorway the hard shoulder should be used

Mark one answer
- [ ] **A.** to answer a mobile phone
- [ ] **B.** when an emergency arises
- [ ] **C.** for a short rest when tired
- [ ] **D.** to check a road atlas

847 For which TWO should you use hazard warning lights?

Mark two answers
- [ ] **A.** When you slow down quickly on a motorway because of a hazard ahead
- [ ] **B.** When you have broken down
- [ ] **C.** When you wish to stop on double yellow lines
- [ ] **D.** When you need to park on the pavement

848 When are you allowed to use hazard warning lights?

Mark one answer
- [ ] **A.** When stopped and temporarily obstructing traffic
- [ ] **B.** When travelling during darkness without headlights
- [ ] **C.** When parked for shopping on double yellow lines
- [ ] **D.** When travelling slowly because you are lost

849
You are on a motorway. A large box falls on to the road from a lorry. The lorry does not stop. You should

Mark one answer
- A. go to the next emergency telephone and inform the police
- B. catch up with the lorry and try to get the driver's attention
- C. stop close to the box until the police arrive
- D. pull over to the hard shoulder, then remove the box

850
There has been an accident. A motorcyclist is lying injured and unconscious. Why should you usually not attempt to remove their helmet?

Mark one answer
- A. Because they may not want you to
- B. This could result in more serious injury
- C. They will get too cold if you do this
- D. Because you could scratch the helmet

851
After an accident, someone is unconscious in their vehicle. When should you call the emergency services?

Mark one answer
- A. Only as a last resort
- B. As soon as possible
- C. After you have woken them up
- D. After checking for broken bones

TIP Don't give casualties anything to eat or drink, or offer them a cigarette. Reassure any injured person and keep them warm while waiting for the ambulance to arrive.

852
An accident casualty has an injured arm. They can move it freely, but it is bleeding. Why should you get them to keep it in a raised position?

Mark one answer
- A. Because it will ease the pain
- B. It will help them to be seen more easily
- C. To stop them touching other people
- D. It will help to reduce the bleeding

853
You are going through a congested tunnel and have to stop. What should you do?

Mark one answer
- A. Pull up very close to the vehicle in front to save space
- B. Ignore any message signs as they are never up to date
- C. Keep a safe distance from the vehicle in front
- D. Make a U-turn and find another route

854
You are going through a tunnel. What should you look out for that warns of accidents or congestion?

Mark one answer
- A. Hazard warning lines
- B. Other drivers flashing their lights
- C. Variable message signs
- D. Areas marked with hatch markings

855
You are going through a tunnel. What systems are provided to warn of any accidents or congestion?

Mark one answer
- A. Double white centre lines
- B. Variable message signs
- C. Chevron 'distance markers'
- D. Rumble strips

856 While driving, a warning light on your vehicle's instrument panel comes on. You should

Mark one answer

- A. continue if the engine sounds alright
- B. hope that it is just a temporary electrical fault
- C. deal with the problem when there is more time
- D. check out the problem quickly and safely

857 You have broken down on a two-way road. You have a warning triangle. You should place the warning triangle at least how far from your vehicle?

Mark one answer

- A. 5 metres (16 feet)
- B. 25 metres (82 feet)
- C. 45 metres (147 feet)
- D. 100 metres (328 feet)

858 You break down on a level crossing. The lights have not yet begun to flash. Which THREE things should you do?

Mark three answers

- A. Telephone the signal operator
- B. Leave your vehicle and get everyone clear
- C. Walk down the track and signal the next train
- D. Move the vehicle if a signal operator tells you to
- E. Tell drivers behind what has happened

859 Your vehicle has broken down on an automatic railway level crossing. What should you do FIRST?

Mark one answer

- A. Get everyone out of the vehicle and clear of the crossing
- B. Phone the signal operator so that trains can be stopped
- C. Walk along the track to give warning to any approaching trains
- D. Try to push the vehicle clear of the crossing as soon as possible

860 Your tyre bursts while you are driving. Which TWO things should you do?

Mark two answers

- A. Pull on the handbrake
- B. Brake as quickly as possible
- C. Pull up slowly at the side of the road
- D. Hold the steering wheel firmly to keep control
- E. Continue on at a normal speed

861 Which TWO things should you do when a front tyre bursts?

Mark two answers

- A. Apply the handbrake to stop the vehicle
- B. Brake firmly and quickly
- C. Let the vehicle roll to a stop
- D. Hold the steering wheel lightly
- E. Grip the steering wheel firmly

862 Your vehicle has a puncture on a motorway. What should you do?

Mark one answer

- **A.** Drive slowly to the next service area to get assistance
- **B.** Pull up on the hard shoulder. Change the wheel as quickly as possible
- **C.** Pull up on the hard shoulder. Use the emergency phone to get assistance
- **D.** Switch on your hazard lights. Stop in your lane

863 Which of these items should you carry in your vehicle for use in the event of an accident?

Mark three answers

- **A.** Road map
- **B.** Can of petrol
- **C.** Jump leads
- **D.** Fire extinguisher
- **E.** First aid kit
- **F.** Warning triangle

864 You are in an accident on a two-way road. You have a warning triangle with you. At what distance before the obstruction should you place the warning triangle?

Mark one answer

- **A.** 25 metres (82 feet)
- **B.** 45 metres (147 feet)
- **C.** 100 metres (328 feet)
- **D.** 150 metres (492 feet)

865 You have broken down on a two-way road. You have a warning triangle. It should be displayed

Mark one answer

- **A.** on the roof of your vehicle
- **B.** at least 150 metres (492 feet) behind your vehicle
- **C.** at least 45 metres (147 feet) behind your vehicle
- **D.** just behind your vehicle

866 You have stalled in the middle of a level crossing and cannot restart the engine. The warning bell starts to ring. You should

Mark one answer

- **A.** get out and clear of the crossing
- **B.** run down the track to warn the signal operator
- **C.** carry on trying to restart the engine
- **D.** push the vehicle clear of the crossing

867 You are on the motorway. Luggage falls from your vehicle. What should you do?

Mark one answer

- **A.** Stop at the next emergency telephone and contact the police
- **B.** Stop on the motorway and put on hazard lights whilst you pick it up
- **C.** Walk back up the motorway to pick it up
- **D.** Pull up on the hard shoulder and wave traffic down

868 You are on a motorway. When can you use hazard warning lights?

Mark two answers

- A. When a vehicle is following too closely
- B. When you slow down quickly because of danger ahead
- C. When you are towing another vehicle
- D. When driving on the hard shoulder
- E. When you have broken down on the hard shoulder

869 You are involved in an accident with another vehicle. Someone is injured. Your vehicle is damaged. Which FOUR of the following should you find out?

Mark four answers

- A. Whether the driver owns the other vehicle involved
- B. The other driver's name, address and telephone number
- C. The make and registration number of the other vehicle
- D. The occupation of the other driver
- E. The details of the other driver's vehicle insurance
- F. Whether the other driver is licensed to drive

870 You have broken down on a motorway. When you use the emergency telephone you will be asked

Mark three answers

- A. for the number on the telephone that you are using
- B. for your driving licence details
- C. for the name of your vehicle insurance company
- D. for details of yourself and your vehicle
- E. whether you belong to a motoring organisation

871 You lose control of your car and damage a garden wall. No one is around. What must you do?

Mark one answer **NI**

- A. Report the accident to the police within 24 hours
- B. Go back to tell the house owner the next day
- C. Report the accident to your insurance company when you get home
- D. Find someone in the area to tell them about it immediately

872 Your engine catches fire. What should you do first?

Mark one answer

- A. Lift the bonnet and disconnect the battery
- B. Lift the bonnet and warn other traffic
- C. Call the breakdown service
- D. Call the fire brigade

873 Before driving through a tunnel what should you do?

Mark one answer

- A. Switch your radio off
- B. Remove any sun-glasses
- C. Close your sunroof
- D. Switch on windscreen wipers

874 You are driving through a tunnel and the traffic is flowing normally. What should you do?

Mark one answer

- A. Use parking lights
- B. Use front spotlights
- C. Use dipped headlights
- D. Use rear fog lights

875 Before entering a tunnel it is good advice to

Mark one answer

- [ ] **A.** put on your sun-glasses
- [ ] **B.** check tyre pressures
- [ ] **C.** change to a lower gear
- [ ] **D.** tune your radio to a local channel

876 You are driving through a tunnel. Your vehicle breaks down. What should you do?

Mark one answer

- [ ] **A.** Switch on hazard warning lights
- [ ] **B.** Remain in your vehicle
- [ ] **C.** Wait for the police to find you
- [ ] **D.** Rely on CCTV cameras seeing you

877 Your vehicle breaks down in a tunnel. What should you do?

Mark one answer

- [ ] **A.** Stay in your vehicle and wait for the police
- [ ] **B.** Stand in the lane behind your vehicle to warn others
- [ ] **C.** Stand in front of your vehicle to warn oncoming drivers
- [ ] **D.** Switch on hazard lights then go and call for help immediately

878 You have an accident while driving through a tunnel. You are not injured but your vehicle cannot be driven. What should you do first?

Mark one answer

- [ ] **A.** Rely on other drivers phoning for the police
- [ ] **B.** Switch off the engine and switch on hazard lights
- [ ] **C.** Take the names of witnesses and other drivers
- [ ] **D.** Sweep up any debris that is in the road

879 When driving through a tunnel you should

Mark one answer

- [ ] **A.** Look out for variable message signs
- [ ] **B.** Use your air-conditioning system
- [ ] **C.** Switch on your rear fog lights
- [ ] **D.** Always use your windscreen wipers

880 What TWO safeguards could you take against fire risk to your vehicle?

Mark two answers

- [ ] **A.** Keep water levels above maximum
- [ ] **B.** Carry a fire extinguisher
- [ ] **C.** Avoid driving with a full tank of petrol
- [ ] **D.** Use unleaded petrol
- [ ] **E.** Check out any strong smell of petrol
- [ ] **F.** Use low-octane fuel

> **TIP** To be confident that you could be of help in an accident, consider taking a course in First Aid from St John Ambulance or St Andrew's Ambulance Association, or from the British Red Cross. You can find local contact numbers in the phone book.

881 You are towing a small trailer on a busy three-lane motorway. All the lanes are open. You must

Mark two answers
- A. not exceed 60mph
- B. not overtake
- C. have a stabilizer fitted
- D. use only the left and centre lanes

882 Any load that is carried on a roof rack MUST be

Mark one answer
- A. securely fastened when driving
- B. carried only when strictly necessary
- C. as light as possible
- D. covered with plastic sheeting

883 You are planning to tow a caravan. Which of these will mostly help to aid the vehicle handling?

Mark one answer
- A. A jockey-wheel fitted to the tow bar
- B. Power steering fitted to the towing vehicle
- C. Anti-lock brakes fitted to the towing vehicle
- D. A stabilizer fitted to the tow bar

884 If a trailer swerves or snakes when you are towing it you should

Mark one answer
- A. ease off the accelerator and reduce your speed
- B. let go of the steering wheel and let it correct itself
- C. brake hard and hold the pedal down
- D. increase your speed as quickly as possible

885 How can you stop a caravan snaking from side to side?

Mark one answer
- A. Turn the steering wheel slowly to each side
- B. Accelerate to increase your speed
- C. Stop as quickly as you can
- D. Slow down very gradually

886 On which TWO occasions might you inflate your tyres to more than the recommended normal pressure?

Mark two answers
- A. When the roads are slippery
- B. When driving fast for a long distance
- C. When the tyre tread is worn below 2mm
- D. When carrying a heavy load
- E. When the weather is cold
- F. When the vehicle is fitted with anti-lock brakes

887 A heavy load on your roof rack will

Mark one answer
- A. improve the road holding
- B. reduce the stopping distance
- C. make the steering lighter
- D. reduce stability

888 Are passengers allowed to ride in a caravan that is being towed?

Mark one answer
- A. Yes if they are over 14
- B. No not at any time
- C. Only if all the seats in the towing vehicle are full
- D. Only if a stabilizer is fitted

889

You are towing a caravan along a motorway. The caravan begins to swerve from side to side. What should you do?

Mark one answer

- A. Ease off the accelerator slowly
- B. Steer sharply from side to side
- C. Do an emergency stop
- D. Speed up very quickly

890

A trailer must stay securely hitched-up to the towing vehicle. What additional safety device can be fitted to the trailer braking system?

Mark one answer

- A. Stabilizer
- B. Jockey wheel
- C. Corner steadies
- D. Breakaway cable

891

Overloading your vehicle can seriously affect the

Mark two answers

- A. gearbox
- B. steering
- C. handling
- D. battery life
- E. journey time

892

Who is responsible for making sure that a vehicle is not overloaded?

Mark one answer

- A. The driver of the vehicle
- B. The owner of the items being carried
- C. The person who loaded the vehicle
- D. The licensing authority

893

Which of these is a suitable restraint for a child under three years?

Mark one answer

- A. A child seat
- B. An adult holding a child
- C. An adult seat belt
- D. A lap belt

894

A child under three years is being carried in your vehicle. They should be secured in a restraint. Which of these is suitable?

Mark one answer

- A. An adult holding a child
- B. A lap belt
- C. A baby carrier
- D. An adult seat belt

TIP There isn't any room for argument here – passengers can't travel in a vehicle that's being towed.

TIP A stabilizer attached to the tow bar can help in making your tow load or trailer more secure.

Section 15 – **Answers to Questions**

ALERTNESS – SECTION 1

1 C	2 BDF	3 C	4 D	5 C	6 C	7 C	8 C	9 B
10 D	11 AC	12 ABCD	13 AD	14 AB	15 AB	16 ABCD	17 C	18 B
19 D	20 B	21 C	22 B	23 B	24 ABE	25 C	26 B	27 B
28 D	29 C	30 C	31 C	32 A	33 D	34 D		

ATTITUDE – SECTION 2

35 D	36 A	37 C	38 B	39 C	40 D	41 D	42 B	43 B
44 BCD	45 ABE	46 A	47 D	48 B	49 A	50 A	51 B	52 A
53 A	54 C	55 A	56 B	57 D	58 D	59 D	60 A	61 A
62 B	63 C	64 A	65 C	66 A	67 C	68 B	69 C	70 DE
71 B	72 D	73 B	74 C	75 D	76 B	77 C	78 A	79 A
80 B	81 A							

SAFETY AND YOUR VEHICLE – SECTION 3

82 B	83 AB	84 ABF	85 BEF	86 C	87 ACF	88 C	89 B	90 A
91 D	92 C	93 D	94 D	95 D	96 A	97 AE	98 D	99 B
100 D	101 D	102 A	103 B	104 BCDF	105 D	106 D	107 BC	108 BC
109 A	110 D	111 C	112 A	113 B	114 B	115 D	116 C	117 D
118 D	119 D	120 B	121 B	122 B	123 D	124 AB	125 ABF	126 ABC
127 ABC	128 BDF	129 D	130 ADE	131 BDF	132 D	133 B	134 CDE	135 B
136 B	137 C	138 B	139 DE	140 A	141 C	142 B	143 D	144 D
145 D	146 B	147 C	148 A	149 B	150 D	151 A	152 C	153 A
154 B	155 AB	156 A	157 D	158 B	159 BCD	160 C	161 CD	162 A
163 A	164 D	165 C	166 B	167 B	168 B	169 D	170 ABE	171 ADE
172 D								

SAFETY MARGINS – SECTION 4

173 D	174 D	175 BC	176 B	177 D	178 D	179 C	180 B	181 BC
182 A	183 ACE	184 B	185 A	186 B	187 A	188 B	189 AE	190 C
191 B	192 C	193 BDEF	194 B	195 D	196 A	197 C	198 A	199 AD
200 C	201 B	202 B	203 B	204 C	205 C	206 B	207 B	208 BC
209 C	210 C	211 B	212 C	213 D	214 BC	215 B	216 ACE	217
218 D	219 D	220 A	221 D	222 BD	223 D	224 B	225 A	22
227 A	228 B							

HAZARD AWARENESS – SECTION 5

229 D	230 CD	231 B	232 C	233 A	234 D	235 ACE	236 D	237 C
238 A	239 C	240 C	241 D	242 B	243 B	244 A	245 A	246 A
247 C	248 C	249 CD	250 A	251 B	252 A	253 C	254 BF	255 B
256 AE	257 A	258 D	259 D	260 C	261 B	262 B	263 C	264 A
265 B	266 B	267 CD	268 B	269 D	270 B	271 A	272 A	273 D
274 A	275 B	276 AE	277 C	278 B	279 BC	280 D	281 B	282 B
283 C	284 D	285 C	286 CD	287 AC	288 AB	289 A	290 A	291 B
292 A	293 ABC	294 C	295 C	296 C	297 ABE	298 C	299 D	300 D
301 C	302 C	303 D	304 ABD	305 ABC	306 D	307 C	308 AB	309 B
310 B	311 CD	312 D	313 ACE	314 ABE	315 A	316 A	317 D	318 D
319 A	320 D	321 A	322 B					

VULNERABLE ROAD USERS – SECTION 6

323 D	324 D	325 C	326 C	327 B	328 D	329 D	330 AD	331 B
332 C	333 D	334 A	335 D	336 D	337 B	338 D	339 B	340 D
341 D	342 C	343 AC	344 C	345 C	346 A	347 D	348 C	349 D
350 ABC	351 C	352 B	353 B	354 AC	355 ABD	356 B	357 D	358 A
359 D	360 A	361 D	362 D	363 A	364 A	365 C	366 C	367 C
368 D	369 ACE	370 D	371 B	372 A	373 C	374 D	375 C	376 C
377 A	378 D	379 D	380 A	381 A	382 B	383 B	384 D	385 C
386 C	387 B	388 C	389 AE	390 D	391 C	392 C	393 B	394 B
395 D	396 D	397 A	398 C	399 C	400 D	401 D	402 B	403 D
404 D	405 B	406 B	407 C					

OTHER TYPES OF VEHICLE – SECTION 7

408 B	409 A	410 A	411 B	412 B	413 D	414 B	415 A	416 BC
417 B	418 D	419 A	420 A	421 A	422 C	423 B	424 B	425 D
426 D	427 D	428 B	429 B	430 B	431 B	432 AC	433 BD	434 B
435 B	436 D							

VEHICLE HANDLING – SECTION 8

438 ACE	439 A	440 CD	441 D	442 A	443 BDF	444 C	445 D
447 DE	448 D	449 B	450 C	451 D	452 C	453 D	454 D
456 C	457 BD	458 BD	459 D	460 B	461 C	462 CE	463 C
5 A	466 A	467 C	468 B	469 ABDF	470 A	471 D	472 B
1 B	475 BD	476 A	477 ACD	478 B	479 A	480 C	481 B
	484 C	485 C	486 A	487 B	488 C	489 D	490 B
	493 D	494 C	495 C	496 C	497 D	498 D	499 A